Endorsements

In a world where we find ourselves distracted by either being too busy doing good or pulled away doing bad, we need to recalibrate our lives to focus on what is best. Chip invites us to connect to God "at the deepest level of our being." Stepping into the thin places needs to become our highest priority in order to become the people God created us to be and make the impact He has created us to make.

—Eric Michael Bryant
Elder, Speaker, and Navigator
Mosaic in Los Angeles
Author, *Not Like Me: A Field Guide for Influencing
a Diverse World*

To an Irish man like me, a thin place is the remote Isle of Iona of the coast of Scotland, where church walls been impregnated with the prayers and tears of devoted saints who have prayed and fasted in desperation to commune with their God. A unique and mystical holy place where it's possible to enter into a closeness to the divine in a way that is truly life transforming. A regular place of annual pilgrimage. Chip in this wonderful book opens our eyes to a virtual thin place, another reality, where God Himself uses the rough and tumble of life as a means to get our attention. After that—all heaven can break out. This book made me

i

hungrier for God, even when the levels of inconvenience and discomfort are at their most extreme.

—Eddie Lyle
Chief Executive Officer
Open Doors UK & Ireland

Thin Places *awakens us to the reality of the Creator's intention to intricately weave Himself into our daily lives. It is loaded with uplifting stories to provide real encouragement when we walk through the "darkest times and thin places" of our lives...A definite must-read.*

—Manny Ohonme
Founder, President, & CEO
Samaritan's Feet International

This treatise by Chip Furr takes you where few books have gone before—to the amazing, transformational place where your world and God's power collide. Get ready for the ride of a lifetime, a kaleidoscope of endless possibilities.

—Jim Buchan
Crosslink Ministries

The first time I heard Chip talking about Thin Places, *I knew it was not only going to be a success but also was something from God. I met Chip several years ago when God "collided" us in a missionary trip and placed us in thin places together. I had the opportunity to know him as a transparent and caring man. While in the mission field I noticed his incredible ability to click immediately with people and their customs, He was always looking for ways to empower people and anxiously desiring to bring about their best. Chip is a man who is writing out of his experience, someone who has walked the walk and talked the talk.*

—Lawrence Otarola
Matrimonio, la Empresa de la Vida International
www.matrimonioempresa.com

Those of us in the industrial, utilitarian West live in a society that increasingly eschews the power and mystery of the narrative. Yet as human beings, we are an amalgam of our life stories, experiences, and existential encounters with mystery. In engaging prose and skillful personal story-telling, Chip Furr reminds us that through disciplined spiritual reflection and faith in God, we discover that our life is not aimlessly wandering in pointless existence, but rather is a purposeful journey that we can direct and submit to the will of a loving God. An encouraging perspective for our time!

—Rev. Dr. Elmo D. Familiaran
Associate Regional Pastor
The American Baptist Churches of New Jersey

Chip's unexpected encounters with God in the thin places that challenge his preconceived notions about life, God, and himself are also a challenge for us! A must-read.

—Jeffrey Watters
Major Chaplain, US Army

When you read this publication you will immediately ask, "Chip, why didn't you put pen to paper (or sit at the keyboard and type!) before now!"

He reminds us early on in the text of the Celtic understanding of "thin places"—those times when we feel especially connected to God and God with us, those times when we experience the transforming power of God. Chip speaks especially into those times in our lives when things can become challenging and desperate. By taking the reader through a captivating journey of faith he is able to show us that God is indeed with us at all times and in all places—even when it might seem to us that we have been abandoned by the one who loves us most.

Each chapter offers a short text at the beginning and a series of thought-provoking questions at the end—questions that can be used as prompts for personal reflection or to facilitate group discussion. Chip's narrative style makes this a compelling read for both those who are just beginning their faith journey and those who are already "on the way." It is no wonder that the subtitle to this publication is "Surprising Collisions Between the Human Spirit and the Presence of God," for from beginning to end Chip recounts stories that show us just amazing our God is.

—Reverend Peter Ball
Church of England
National Youth Adviser

thin places

thin places

Surprising

Collisions Between

the Human SPIRIT and

the PRESENCE OF GOD

CHIP FURR

DEVELOPMENT SERVICES, INC

Oviedo, Florida

Published by HigherLife Development Services, Inc.
400 Fontana Circle
Building 1 – Suite 105
Oviedo, FL 32765
(407) 563-4806
www.ahigherlife.com

Cover Design: r2c Design — Rachel Lopez
First Edition
10 11 12 13 — 9 8 7 6 5 4 3 2 1
Printed in the United States of America

Dedication

Thin *Places* would have never been written if not for my wife of twenty-nine years and best friend, Cheery. This book is about journeys encompassing twenty-five years of missions all around the world. The first mission trip that I ever embarked on as a seventeen-year-old is the trip that introduced me to her in Manila, Philippines.

Missions from the beginning has blessed me with the greatest gift a man could ever have: a wife who believes in me when nothing is going right. Cheery encouraged me when the nights were long and the words ran out. When I felt at a loss for what the next step in life might be, she placed within me the thought to write and to strive to be only what God had for me, not for others. It's all about perspective. She believed in me more than I did.

No one understands me more,

loves me more,

shares the pain with me more,

and is more content to play a supportive role in all of what God calls me to do than Cheery is. The reality is she has been the voice of reason and has kept me grounded throughout ministry. This book would not be here today if not for her.

I love you, Sweetie.

This book is dedicated to the entire CLIMB team and the ministry it stands for: to hold at the core of all values the goal of serving and helping others who cannot help themselves. CLIMB Ministries is the greatest missional organization I could envision serving. I love you guys…

To my father-in-law, Rev. Moley Familiaran, who has been with the LORD for years. You always told me to tell the stories and dedicate my life's experiences to the calling of God. You were right. I miss you…

Table of Contents

Chapters/Entries

Foreword

We suffer from a lot of things in life—disappointment, illness, loss of a job, broken relationships, you name it. But I think many of us suffer a more silent, insidious threat, a condition that robs us of the satisfying aroma of life, the lush, colorful living we long for. When you get right down to the core of what's wrong, the answer is surprising. We're simply *bored*.

This has always seemed ironic to me. How can people be *bored* amid our high-tech, high-speed, high-definition world? Why do we find "nothing to watch" on TV when our cable box brings us over two hundred channels? And why are so many people experiencing withering relationships in a world where they can "socially network" with hundreds of "friends" on Facebook or Twitter?

Clearly, something is missing. Our technology may be "living color" and "high-definition," but our lives too often are gray and purposeless.

God created us for so much more than this. Biblical characters faced many difficult circumstances—how would *you* like to be thrown into a fiery furnace or lions' den?—but you didn't hear them complaining of boring or purposeless lives. Life was an adventure, as it should be for us.

But most of life's adventures are discovered in the *thin places*. You know, those faint, indefinable moments where we sense something beyond ourselves is at work. Life becomes a thrill ride, a scary yet exhilarating roller coaster, when our natural world and supernatural collide—and that's exactly what these thin places are all about.

If you've come to the point of recognizing a void in your life, you may be on the verge of something very exciting: a life-changing encounter with God's presence in one of life's thin places. Are you ready to step off the path of the familiar, the safe and sanguine, to experience the wild unknown richness of God's love and intervention in your life? Open your eyes. Thin places where the divine touches your humanity are all around you.

You may not like the "place" you find yourself in right now, but I have good news: this book will give you a glimpse of God's supernatural possibilities for your future. You don't need to remain stuck in a drab, predictable world of motion without meaning. Chip Furr is beckoning you to a higher place, a thin place where safety gives way to satisfaction and significance.

Chip Furr has journeyed through life's thin places, and he tells you about some of them in this book. Chip's an awesome storyteller. As you read of his unexpected encounters with the divine, I believe you will find hope for your own journey. No matter what kind of "place" you find yourself in today, I'm convinced God can meet you there. There are thin places waiting for you…maybe today. Just open your eyes and your heart—and get ready!

—Mark Batterson
Pastor of National Community Church in Washington DC
Author of *In a Pit with a Lion on a Snowy Day: How to Survive and Thrive When Opportunity Roars* and *Wild Goose Chase: Reclaim the Adventure of Pursuing God*

Acknowledgments

To my dear brother in Christ, Ted Ake, whom I met years ago at a local church and have shared life's stories with up until today. Ted moved away several years ago to follow what God called him to do. We stay in touch often, and Ted has been a constant supporter of my family and CLIMB for years. Thanks, Ted, for all you did to make this book a reality. Thanks for being there for me each and every day. You have the heart of a lion and are willing to serve anytime, anywhere. Love you and your family always.

To Nan Henderson, who has believed in me and what God had for me every step of the journey. I remember when we first met at the men's shelter. You've been my second mom ever since. The prayers you prayed for me allowed me to see God at work when all other circumstances in my life seemed to be dismal. Know that the time you spent with me in the worst of times made today and this book project the greatest dream come true. I love you more than you know.

To Ken and Denise Hammond. Years ago in perhaps one of the deepest, darkest places in my life, you two offered help that gave Cheery and me a fresh look at the provisions of God. God used you both in a mighty way. Without that then, this book would not be here now. Thanks for believing and loving us when we had nothing else. May the newness of life and joy always be your guide. Love ya…

To Bill Ringer, who has stuck with me from the old gym days of running indoor soccer. Brother, can you believe we have come this far? Thanks for taking the ride with me. You win the "Iron Man" award. You're the best!

To Charlie Noggle and those early morning Saturday walks at the school. You have been the constant ear for my ongoing struggles. I thought the book would be impossible to achieve, but you believed all along. Your words and phone calls every day inspired me to be more than I could be. Love ya, brother.

To Jim Buchan, who encouraged me every step of the way. You are one of the most brilliant writers and editors I know. Thanks for those calls late at night to ask about the book and keep me focused. Your belief in my simple writing skills stretched me beyond what I ever imagined. Know that you're loved and appreciated.

To David Welday. You pushed me to believe in myself. The prayer time we had in Los Angeles caused me to get serious about the book. Thanks for those great words. You are the brother that I always wished for.

To Chris Maxwell, who edited this book to perfection. You are more than just an editor to me; you're the long-lost best friend I never had. Your text messages are the most encouraging. Thanks for believing.

To Mac Willet, who read the original manuscript and formed questions that make us all think deep within. You're awesome.

To Mark Batterson, who spent time with me when he had other things to do. He encouraged me to write and to shoot the DVD for the book, and he said this book would touch many. Thanks, Mark. Your personal time and e-mails were the medicine I needed at the right times. Thanks for inspiring me in this project.

To Kendall Lloyd, who has been with me since "dirt." My brother, where in the world would CLIMB be if not for you? Thanks for all the cyberspace—the Web building, blog producing, word pressing, uploading, downloading, databasing, and e-tapping voice of reason. When I said, "Can it be done?" you said, "I'll make it happen." And you did, every time. Your gifts continue to bless CLIMB, and your passion to serve is off the charts. Thanks for always being there.

To Gary Davies, who from the beginning believed in me and what God was going to do through CLIMB. You gave us the fuel to leave the ground. Thanks for taking the leap with us. You said God would bless this ministry. Boy, were you right!

Introduction:
The Journey

Just show up and things will happen.

—Mother Theresa

Life is full of *thin places*. There's a narrow line between life and death, peace and war, success and failure, walking with God or being oblivious to His presence. *Thin place* is an old Celtic term. The Irish defined *thin place* as a place where we feel connected to God at the deepest level of our being. A place where we can touch the seen and the unseen at the same time if for only a split second.

What are the thin places? Marcus J. Borg, in *The Heart of Christianity*, writes that a thin place is where "we can behold God, experience the one in whom we live, all around us and in us."[1]

Life is defined by our discoveries—and decisions—in life's thin places.

Will we seize the moment...or miss it?

---

1   Marcus J. Borg, *The Heart of Christianity* (New York: HarperOne, 2004), 156.

Will we discern the wonder of an unexpected event…or grumble that our plans were interrupted?

Will our meeting with a stranger turn out to be a life-changing encounter… or a missed opportunity?

Think back.

Remember a thin place along your journey.

While it may have been the most fantastic adventure you've ever experienced, it probably never appeared on your To-Do list or five-year plan. Perhaps it only lasted a few brief moments, yet it changed your trajectory for a lifetime.

If you've encountered God's wonder in a thin place, you probably remember the exact place you were, who you were with, the sights, the smells. Many thin places occur when times are tough, when our backs are against the wall. We certainly didn't *choose* these circumstances. But they came our way.

Are you ready to join me in a thrilling—though sometimes painful— exploration of the thin places of your life? I invite you.

This journey is for you *if…*

…you feel like you've been hit by an oncoming train and are struggling to understand what has happened.

…you seek deliverance from a life of vice—or just a life of mediocrity and boredom.

…you're craving a high-definition life, even in a low-definition world.

Let me explain why life's thin places are a key to transformation as we prepare ourselves for this journey.

God wants to take your life from black and white…transform it into color… to high definition. Instead of drowning in monotony and purposelessness, He's beckoning you to enter a thrill ride of joyous discovery and transformation.

This kind of transformation begins as you embrace the thin places with curiosity and adventure. Yes, curiosity. Yes, adventure. Think of those words, of those experiences. That experience requires allowing God to engage your imagination with His creativity.

Reviving your old dreams.

Giving you new ones.

In some abstract way, we have to abandon ourselves to God. Forgetting our habits of thinking. Choosing to imagine. Imagination changes the way we look at the world and the world looks at us. It takes us to places—thin places where the divine is all around us.

In *Wild Goose Chase,* Mark Batterson writes about thin places as where "natural and supernatural worlds collide."[2] Leighton Ford, in *The Attentive Life,* mentions that the ancient Celts referred to thin places as "where heaven and earth seem very near each other."[3]

What does this collision look like?

Simple meets confusing.

Predictability meets unpredictability.

Human logic meets the unfathomable and often bewildering purposes of
   God.

---

2   Mark Batterson, *Wild Goose Chase: Reclaim the Adventure of Pursuing God* (Colorado Springs, CO: Multnomah Books, 2008), 46.
3   Leighton Ford, *The Attentive Life: Discerning God's Presence in All Things* (Westmont, IL: InterVarsity Books, 2008), 188.

Imagine the collision Peter, James, and John felt on the mountain during an experience known as the Transfiguration. Jesus took them to a thin place where the veil between this world and the other world was so thin that it became easy to step into.

There is a world beyond ours that's within our reach if we allow our faculty of reason to be suspended for a short time.

If you are still trying to figure out God on a strictly rational basis, I wish you well. However, it's sobering that even the apostle Paul reached a point where his human understanding collided with divine revelation:

> O the depth of the riches of wisdom and knowledge of
> God!
> How unsearchable his judgments
> and how inscrutable his ways!
> "For who has known the mind of the Lord,
> or who has been his counselor?"
> "Or who has given a gift to him
> that he might be repaid?"
> For from him and through him and to him are all things.
> To him be the glory for ever! Amen. (Rom. 11:33-36)

So, what is this universal yearning, this transformation, this renewal? What are these thin places?

Transformation is a yearning of every human heart—whether people are consciously aware of their yearning or not.

Listen closely, and you'll witness this universal yearning in everything from pop songs to TV commercials, and from billboards to magazine covers. Movies, perhaps more than any other current medium, reflect the human craving for transformation—for a life change so significant that it impacts the surrounding world.

I remember the movie *Raiders of the Lost Ark*.[4] More than any other movie of that time, it was the adventure of adventures. Scary as it may have been, I wanted to live the life of an Indiana Jones. A life that takes you to places unknown, meeting people from all corners of the world. Some of these individuals may seem like characters from a comic book—appearing and disappearing. The fedora and the bullwhip seemed appealing and adventurous.

Indiana taught at the local university as a professor of archaeology. When the bell rang and the class was dismissed, Indiana took trips that at any time could cost him his life. His students thought he was home grading papers. He lived a double life in a sense. On the one hand, he invested in the lives of his students. On the other hand, he was pulled by a higher power that called him to live life on the edge. Seriously, I teach at the local school every day. My students have no idea that I travel to all corners of the world when the school is on a break or out for the summer.

So, let me tell you some of my story. As I invite you to learn lessons from life's thin places, here is a little history of my journey.

What? Me? Maybe? You think? BANG! COLLISION!

I've asked each of these expressions of doubt over a period of time. It all led to what you now have in your hands—a book that I had to be convinced to write. Convinced in my own mind that it needed to be shared with others.

I suppose I need to begin by telling you about a "collision" that actually pushed me over the edge to begin writing this book. I had struggled with questions each time I thought about typing.

---

4   *Raiders of the Lost Ark*, directed by Steven Spielberg (Hollywood, CA: Paramount Pictures, 1981).

Would it be read by anyone but me?

Would I have the talent and time to write it?

How much would it cost to publish?

Was I just wasting my time and the time of others?

Others would have to buy into the dream of mine in writing this book for it to ever get done. I struggled. Each day I wondered if it would ever happen. God sent people into my life with words of encouragement. It was greatly appreciated. They knew the book I was thinking about writing, and so they stayed on me about writing it. I could not ask for more. The doubt came from me and in my own lack of ability and strength. Success or failure rested on me and me alone is what I thought. As long as I thought that way, the book would seem like a mountain I could not CLIMB.

Until one day a collision happened. "A Message from God!"

It changed my whole entire outlook on writing this book.

This collision, this thin place, happened in a local cleaners while picking up shirts I had dropped off months before. I had forgotten all about them. I only remembered to pick them up because I was leaving for a conference in California.

I walked in as usual. Same faces behind the counter. I'd known those people since I was a kid. My father brought me there and sat me up on the counter while they fetched his clothes. I was probably around five years old. Now, in my forties, they know my face even better.

"Mister Chip! Where have you been? I've been looking for you for months; five months. I've been waiting on you to come through that door," she said.

Of course, I figured that they had lost my shirts. After all, five months? They aren't responsible for the shirts after that much time. I clearly had passed that limit.

"I'm sorry. I've been traveling. In fact, I need my shirts so I can pack them to leave again."

"Mister Chip. I have something to tell you, and I've been waiting till you got here."

To me it sounded bad. Not only might my shirts be lost but perhaps something worse she needed to tell me about my son—he also took his clothes to them.

"Is it my son?" I asked.

"Nope! Where's your ticket? Let me get the shirts and then I'll tell you," she said, exasperated.

As she put my shirts on the counter, she began to share what she'd been waiting to reveal. But you must know this—she knew nothing about me other than I was a pastor in missions and lived down the block with a wonderful wife and son.

"Mister Chip, the Lord has something for me to tell you." For the first time she had my complete and undivided attention. I was not even aware she was a spiritual woman. I was shocked but eager to hear what she had to say. And then the collision happened.

"You know that book you're supposed to write? Well, the Lord told me to tell you to write it. Don't worry about anything. You see, you've been waiting. Don't worry about how many books you're going to sell. Your job is just to write it—the selling isn't your problem."

I felt like one of the still, solid wax figures in a museum. She had no idea about any book. Why would I tell her? It made no sense to tell her. And then she continued.

"And your ministry, the one you've been working on for years and traveling around—well, the Lord said don't worry about that either. He's going to bless it. More than you can imagine. You've been worried about that, haven't you? It's been holding you back, scared to step out and let God worry about what happens to your ministry and the book. So go on, what are you waiting on?"

There was no money in the CLIMB's account. So in reality, she hit the spiritual nail on the head twice.

My face was a long pause. I just stood there and looked at her.

She said, "What's the matter? Does that not make sense?"

"It does," I replied.

But now what? I had heard from people close to me to sit down and just write. Friends that I trusted. Two editor friends called me periodically to ask if I had started writing.

But the doubt. It just kept creeping in.

Has that ever happened to you?

You can't move due to insecurity in yourself, so nothing gets done. They call it procrastination. Let's call it what it is: *fear!*

I didn't trust what I might be able to write. It was all about what *I* could do, not what God was going to do with the book to encourage others. As long as it remains about us and our abilities, fear will paralyze us.

But a person on the fringes of friendship—you know the kind—was charging me with this task. They are not really in your six degrees of separation of information, and you see them every now and then. Her straightforward words of conviction had more impact on me than my closest friends I deeply trusted. For me there seems to be a difference when a stranger knows your plans and confirms them as if she was reading your mail. Friends know and are expected to encourage. But someone who knows nothing about your personal plans uncovers them without a hint and challenges you to do what you already know.

Her words had to be coming from God. Her words had no attachments. It was a clear message with no expected kickbacks for her other than this: she had a message from God and here it is.

Every time I go to the cleaners to get my clothes, she is there.

"Well, did you start?"

For the first time in my life I was able to say, "I sure did."

And you know what? The day after this encounter, CLIMB received the largest check it had ever received.

She was right on *His* promise again. Every time I go by this place of business, I never look at it the same way I used to. It's a great place, "Coachman Cleaners." It represents a thin place where God spoke through a passionate woman behind the counter and I listened.

What about you?

I'm simple. I live in a simple house with simple means. I own nothing. I'm not a recognizable figure to anyone. No one would know my name. I'm not on YouTube. I have trouble keeping up with my own blog. I haven't written a book before. But in writing there is a dynamic that you can't control. You tell the story, the truth, the experiences. You let the story tell itself. It lets you be who you really are.

Writing this book was deep and personal. Wounds healed as I concentrated on two things: God and human beings. That's really what life is all about for me. The journey God has planned for me and the people I meet along that path.

What else is there but God and people? People have shaped me and inspired me when I felt like quitting. Friends inspired me to get off my butt and try again. And to try again after failure.

Friends ask the hard questions. Yet even when the answer is different than they expected, they walk the journey of thin places with you.

What about you?

Have you ever desired to leave Kansas like Dorothy and imagine what life would be like if you just dared? Dared in such a way that you are open to wherever the yellow brick road leads? To lean into life and not be on the defensive? To explore, challenge, and be available to God?

Encounters and conversations with people you never imagined.

Dorothy met four characters that were all different yet desired something in life. She played a huge role in how they found what they were looking for.

What about you?

Imagine someone out there waiting for you to live this life seeking the thin places so they too can find Oz, so they too can find God. What we need to keep in mind is that Dorothy was always a click away from where she came. Which really means God is only a click away in the other direction.

God is that close.

Within arms' reach.

In his book *The Grand Weaver*, Ravi Zacharias claims that "the Christian walk involves all three areas of life—the spiritual, the practical, and the logical."[5] He goes on to say that these are about "your hopes, your dreams, and your calling."[6] I agree.

But, when in a really thin place, where heaven and earth seem to meet and you are in the middle, logic goes right out the window. You are left with the

5   Ravi Zacharias, *The Grand Weaver: How God Shapes Us through the Events in Our Lives* (Grand Rapids, MI: Zondervan, 2007), 63.
6   Ibid., 79.

spiritual dimension to navigate the road ahead. Sometimes this may seem as if you're driving in a mystical fog that has only faith as a heading.

Mark Batterson says, "Faith is not logical. But it isn't illogical either. Faith is Theological. It does not ignore reality; it just adds God into the equation."[7]

When God is in the equation, life works.

He's all-in! Are you?

No chips left in our corner. Are we betting everything on Him?

Remember: It's the journey that shapes who we are—not the end result.

To me... a thin place always looks like a road of possibilities.

Chip Furr, Lead Pastor
The Climb, Inc.
P. O. Box 11678
Charlotte, NC 28220
E-mail: chip@theclimb.org
Web site: www.theclimb.org

---

7   Batterson, *Wild Goose Chase,* 79.

Entry #1

An Angel and an Old Oak Tree

After these things, God tested Abraham.

—Genesis 22:1a

And you shall remember all the way which the LORD your God
has led you these forty years in the wilderness, that he might
humble you, testing you to know what was in your heart.

—Deuteronomy 8:2

In 1999, tornados hit the states of Oklahoma and Texas with some of the worst twisters ever recorded. I remember a news report saying the twisters that rolled through the small town of Moore, Oklahoma, were of a class F6 tornado.

Funny thing about a class F6 tornado—there's no such thing.

Tornados only go up to class F5. A class F5 is a tornado that has the capability to register 250 miles per hour at the core of the funnel where most of the damage is generated. These twisters rearrange landscape like a giant blender.

Much of what was shown of this small town just outside of Oklahoma City was pure devastation.

This year was a particularly bad year for weather in the United States; mudslides in California, snowstorms in the Northeast, and torrential rain in the upper Northwest. As we in Charlotte, North Carolina, read about all the happenings, First Baptist Church decided to charter a bus and drive to Oklahoma City to offer any assistance that might be needed.

There were forty-five of us. We left from the back of the church parking lot for a twenty-three-hour drive with no scheduled stops other than taking on fuel and having a bite to eat.

I'll never forget arriving in Oklahoma City. One of the guys was telling a funny story to make the time pass. Laughter radiated all through the bus, and sometimes it drowned out the snoring from the back of the bus.

"Are you kidding me?" That was all I remember being said.

No laughter or talking. Just silence.

Staring out the left side of the bus, we could see the landscape had dramatically changed. From a flat and green countryside, it was as if a mammoth bulldozer drove across about ten miles of terrain. The path of destruction that came diagonally across the six-lane highway leading into Oklahoma City was a devastating sight. As we reached the church to camp there for the week, the mood was somber.

I personally had never witnessed the leftover path of what a tornado can do. I remember a huge tree where only half of it was in the direct path of the tornado. The other half was as if it was still sitting in someone's backyard, full of life, never being touched. What a contrast. One side stripped of all the leaves; the other side as beautiful as ever, seemingly not shedding a leaf.

Our team stayed on the second floor of the First Baptist Church of Moore, Oklahoma—across the street of one of the most catastrophic sights I have ever seen. Every house was leveled. Not just damaged. Completely gone. There was no way to tell where the neighborhood started and ended. I watched the people walk around as if they were searching for their own street signs. They might as well have been on the moon. They picked up pieces of personal belongings whenever possible: pictures, clothes, toys, anything that reminded them of what life was like just a month ago. In a moment, in an unexpected event, their lives forever changed.

We spent our first night in the church and woke the next day to view in horror what we were hoping had been just a dream. The effect looked even more profound than the first time we saw it. What had actually happened several weeks before was sinking into our minds.

Our first full day was spent rearranging all the supplies people and organizations had donated to the community. Food. Nonperishables. Clothing. Batteries. Chainsaws. For the most part, it all sat in the back parking lot of the church. It was under a tent supplied by a local college that would accommodate some 10,000 people. Except, this time, it was used as the central location for all material sent from around the country. It took the team most of the day to consolidate the donations.

As the next day dawned, the team located the American Red Cross tent several miles down the street in another church parking lot. We went hoping to be of assistance to anyone.

Both churches in this specific location went undamaged, untouched. We met people who told their personal stories of loss during the violent storms. I had lunch with a lady; she lost not only all her property but her husband also. He was sucked up in the funnel that ravaged their small community.

I cried with her as she retold her story probably for the twentieth time. Imagine replaying that over and over. The pain of that moment never goes away. Some say you just learn to accept and deal with it over time. I'm not so sure.

As I sat at the Red Cross tent, a local farmer walked in and asked where we were from. I told him, Charlotte.

"Ya'll come to help out?" His face looked bewildered and tired. He wondered if we had been approached to do any work or cleanup for the community. I said no. He asked me, "Ya'll roofers?" Personally, I had only been on a roof once in my life back home. He explained to our team that the church was some distance away and needed another roof. Crazy thing, though, this church was in the middle of nowhere. You ever heard of the Sea of Tranquility? Yep! Might as well be on the moon. Even if the town had still been there, it was nowhere visible on a decent map. A GPS would most likely bark back at you and say, "Where?"

This tornado had come through the town and destroyed everything—everything except the church. However, the roof was missing, and church service could not be held Sunday without the roof. Sunday was six days away. My question was, who would be there to attend?

But…I said, "I'm in if I can convince the other guys to do it." They didn't flinch. Well, a week of uncertainty turned into a week of solid work and dedication. Let the "faith" lesson begin.

I remember what God had done for me in the past.

But I was not ready for the visit and lessons that were about to happen.

Our ten men woke up early to make the trip to this remote church location. I mean, hours away. No food. Very little water. Only what we could carry. Loading the church van for the three-hour commute, we found that room for food and water was extremely limited. We had to take tools and material that would take every inch of space. The food and water packed on our laps wouldn't sustain ten men in one-hundred-degree heat twelve hours a day on a roof.

As the sun stretched to rise and darkness still hovered, all the guys met in the parking lot. Not much conversation. Heck, why would there be? We didn't really know what awaited us on the other side; anxiety sometimes turns quiet. The quiet leads to the fear of not knowing what's down the path.

"Hey, Clarence, we don't have enough water to last the day," I said. I thought I would ask the obvious, you know, break the silence. "Are we crazy?!"

"Faith, my brother…faith," he responded.

I've lived on faith most of my spiritual life. Faith and hope are things believed in that remain unseen. I get that. But actually putting it into motion is something different.

I couldn't see a thing!

It made no sense. High Oklahoma heat and little water is not a situation I had longed for. My first lesson from God was: *remember*. In fact, my professor in seminary always told his students that you could sum up the entire Old Testament in one word: *remember*. Remember what God had done for the Israelites. Remember.

This is what I remembered. Having watched my share of National Geographic shows, I knew one simple thing: water we had to have. You can't last long without it.

Clarence was from West Africa and had lived by faith in God all his life. Growing up in a country torn by civil war, he and his family knew God was all they had. To Clarence, three hours into an Oklahoma countryside was just another exercise in God's ongoing trials and the testing of our faith.

The van arrived some three hours later. The town was destroyed. Only the church structure atop the hill was all that was left. The roof was gone, just like they had said. Another company had delivered some of the supplies that we needed to start and finish the job.

Climbing the ladder, I went to the highest point. It was a sight I'll never forget. All was gone, wiped clean from the face of the earth.

Supplies began coming up the ladder. The mercury was also rising. Quickly. By 10:00 a.m., it was in the nineties. Water? What about water? We took a break at 10:30 a.m.; most of the water was gone. And the majority of the work was still in front of us.

"Clarence, I told you this would happen; now what?"

His simple response was, "Faith, my brother."

Have you ever thought about the depth of your faith?

As a follower in Christ, did you ever imagine how far you would go or could be tested by God to discover the answer to this question? I had always understood that to follow God, faith was internal. It surfaced when needed. Well, in the end, maybe that's true. But it's the journey and testing of that faith that awakens the spirit in the depths of a truly committed follower. God is not so much interested in the external. He is deeply interested in the internal.

Faith was dripping away like a faucet with a leak. It was hot. We were in the middle of nowhere. No water. No food. And a local congregation relying on us to complete the job by Sunday. All we had to rely on? God.

Is that enough?

Have you ever noticed God does His best convincing in the avenues of life's journey when He's the only one left for you to have any faith in? You've thought about all worldly possibilities. They didn't work. "Might as well try God," we say.

The *faith lesson* usually comes when the circumstances are bigger than you.

If you can control the event, there's no faith required.

What was I looking for? Predictability. Playing it safe. Is that you?

Imagine if Moses or Abraham would have used this excuse when called by God. Abraham would have stayed home. Moses would have purchased beachfront property with a great view of the Red Sea he would never cross.

As the work continued, the mercury was rising. The roof was covered with things to be done and little energy to do it. Water was now sparse with a long day, a long week, staring back. My mind had been right all along. Clarence was wrong. This *faith thing* that works sometimes wasn't working. The lack of water proved it. Our thirst proved it.

Or was there more? Sometimes God tests in the middle, sometimes in the end, sometimes in the beginning. Read Deuteronomy 8. God tested Abraham in the very beginning. The external was not in question. The internal was. God had already performed miracles in Abraham's life; Isaac was born to a woman ninety years old. Abraham knew deep inside God was who He said He was. That God could do what He said He could do. But sometimes we forget. Sometimes we disbelieve. Sometimes we doubt God's ability to do what He said. Such was the case with me. This was my lesson.

God constantly calls us to keep moving forward in our faith. To do this God will instantly challenge us without warning. We haven't arrived if faith is natural or easy. We aren't learning if we only have stories about faith from the distant past or future. Do we have faith today? In our present heat and thirst and doubt, do we believe?

Faith was almost a comical subject as I smoldered on the roof. Could we drill? Any other ideas? Knowing driving the van back to pick up water was a six-hour-turnaround was knowing enough. How could it happen?

Well, at eleven o'clock something happened.

I looked into the distance, feeling the heat radiating from the ground like an oven. I could see a figure. A person. And that person seemed to be walking in our direction. He came from nowhere. Nothing behind him. No town; no house; no place within miles and miles. He came closer and closer. The closer he walked, the more all the guys became interested. Who was he? Where was he coming from?

Finally, he arrived in the churchyard wearing a hat, black overalls, and a white T-shirt. My guess? Around seventy years old. He had not one sweat mark. We were dripping. It was like he came out of nowhere. Before we could ask him a question, he asked.

"Where ya'll from?"

"Charlotte, North Carolina," we said.

"Ya'll going to be here long?"

"All week," I said.

His face turned to the side as if he was looking for something. He scanned the countryside and looked far off into the distance. All of us on the roof joined him just out of curiosity. He again looked up at us as he stood in one place. Then came this question that got my attention.

"Ya'll have any food and water?"

Where does your mind go now? The two things we didn't have and desperately needed? Food and water.

But he didn't have any either. He carried nothing with him. His hands seemed rough, and he looked like a person that knew something we didn't. He continued to look across the landscape as if he were expecting a friend. Finally, I said, "We have no water." Food wasn't all that important to me at the time.

He said, "Well, in about three hours there will be a truck coming through. Do you see the large oak tree at the bottom of the hill? It's beside a stream of water."

We all squinted, looking for the tree. It was big but a long way off. "Yep, we see it."

"The truck will pull up right there. It will have a tent and all the food and water you can take. But you have to wait. It won't arrive until around 3:00 p.m."

Without another word, mysteriously, he turned and walked back in the same direction that he came. He seemed different. He was friendly, but something did not add up. He mentioned nothing about the storms. He said not a word about his family. Acting as if questions pointed his way weren't important, he focused more on our dilemma.

He disappeared into the landscape far into the distance. He was gone. Vanished.

Hours passed and the heat picked up. The clock ticked near 3:00. We were all anticipating something. Just not sure what.

"Hey, Clarence, what do you think?" I asked. "Any water coming?"

Clarence was a faithful person that kept things in perspective. His faith never wavered—water or no water, he was ready for what would or wouldn't happen.

Life sometimes requires us to have faith in the most uncanny circumstances.

When even faith itself seems illogical.

Let's face it, faith has its parameters. A wall that represents the end of the line and has a blinking neon light that says, "Faith ends here." You just don't go past it. That's where I was. Standing at the wall of impossible.

"Faith, brother, faith."

It was almost laughable to me. But I admired Clarence for his courage. God tests the heart, I guess. What we say and what we are willing to go through are miles apart, right?

The clock turned to 3:00. The oak tree in the far distance stood alone. My heart turned to stone. I felt the whole thing was a joke, as if God was standing there beside me shaking His head, saying, "You still don't get, do you? I have been with you through the desert, and you still doubt."

Then it happened!

One of the largest trucks I had ever seen pulled up beside the oak tree in the distance. Just like the man said. They began to pull out all kinds of tents, just like the man said. They had bathroom facilities, just like the man said. The food began to smell great, and the water was being prepared in buckets of ice, just like the man said. Right down to the last nugget of information, this guy hit the mark. It all happened just like he said. I was scared to look at Clarence. Finally, I glanced his way. He smiled. Just smiled. His smile was saying he never doubted.

We all came off the roof and began walking to the oasis. It was like an oasis in the middle of the desert. I walked up to one of the people cooking the food and setting up tables. I just had to ask about the stranger who told us about them coming. So, I asked, "Who is in charge?"

The gentlemen motioned me to the lady in the white apron beside the water. I walked over and introduced myself, telling her why we were out in that remote location. She didn't seem surprised by what I was telling her as she continued her setup of tables.

I asked her about the man in the dark overalls and hat. "He had been here some three hours ago and told our team that you would arrive around at this time next to the large oak tree."

She stopped instantly. "What man?"

I repeated myself and described him.

She stood and looked at me. Puzzled. Somewhat amused.

I asked, "What seems so funny?"

She said, "That's impossible that anyone would know we were coming here."

"Why?"

"Our plans changed, and we were to be in another location miles from here. This site had not been chosen for us."

"When did you know the location had changed?"

"About an hour ago," she said.

"That's impossible! Three hours ago this man had told us your team would be here."

"What man? We have no one else out here but those you see. We only knew recently that we needed to be here in this spot."

For the rest of the week we had all the food and water we could ever want. Not just a little. All we wanted. It the most remote location I have ever been in. This is what I can remember:

All we could ever want!

That is what I remember.

Oh, I still remember the man in the black overalls. It feels like yesterday.

God comes to us in all kinds of forms. He ministers to us in the most unlikely of places. Lessons are learned and relearned. Especially in the desert.

Faith is checked on. Faith is challenged. Faith asks many questions of us. Even the ones who claim to have unshakeable faith Christ will test.

I remember how God had led me through my life, and now I was humbled again by God. I remember the old oak tree that rested beside the stream—the still waters of the Almighty.

Faith is not about how much. Faith is about knowing God will act, God will come through, God will do what He has always promised if we have the faith of a mustard seed. It's about unseen things and a personal conviction that it will happen. Whatever "it" is, "it" will happen.

God comes in all kinds of forms. A burning bush, a pillar of fire, a cloud that moves in the day.

And a man without a name.

A man from far away never to be seen again.

I only met that man in the black overalls once. Or maybe I meet Him every day.

SEEKING THE THIN PLACES...

1. **Do you think angels exist within our world?** If so, do they break into human history? Why or why not?

2. **We all have a place where faith no longer seems possible.** Recall the last situation in your life when your faith ran out. What was the cause?

3. **Have you ever encountered an angel?** Did you know it then or realize it now?

Entry #2

You Couldn't Stop It

All things truly wicked start from an innocence.

—Ernest Hemingway

Charleston, South Carolina, is one hot place in the dead of summer. "Quaint" would come close to describing it: cobblestone streets and weeping willows have stood there since the Civil War. Tourist and history buffs blanket most of the streets all year long. There is so much to see and observe that one cannot cover it all in one visit.

One of the attractions in the popular southern city of Charleston is the horse-and-carriage ride. Carriages of different sizes and shapes carry as many as fifteen people around the city through the local streets. At times it's as if the entire city were an oil canvas that's come to life. You pass by huge houses that have stood the test of time as hooves from the horses hit the pavement.

One summer my family decided to meet in Charleston for the weekend to discover the Old South southern style. It was the hottest day I can remember. I promised everyone I would set up the carriage ride for the afternoon. The temperature was in the mid-nineties. The humidity felt like a moist, hot blanket. Our family met at the stables where they keep the horses and carriages. There were thirteen of us. We had to be loaded into the largest carriage.

We waited for the *one* horse to be hitched to the carriage. One of the other horses was taking a break, lying down as if he were in a king-size bed. He was inside the stall, and as I leaned over to look more closely, the driver said, "He is the biggest horse we have."

"How many do you have?" I asked.

"We have a total of twenty that we rotate," he said.

I felt concerned for the health of the horse. He pulls the carriage for hours. Though they are treated well and the drivers are very aware of the conditions and take every precaution to ensure that the heat does not exhaust the horse, I was concerned.

My observations? It was hot. The weight wasn't light.

"It seems that the horses would tire long before the day was over," I said.

"You mean from the heat?" the driver said.

"Yep." I was concerned about the weight too. Fifteen people piling on? WOW! And the route that these horses take is over three miles. "It must be tough pulling this carriage through the streets," I said.

"Not really. The horse for the most part doesn't even know the carriage is behind him. You could pull it," he said.

I laughed as if the joke was on me. "No, really, you can pull it," he quickly responded.

He pointed to the carriage and said, "Pick up the poles and lean forward." I thought the whole time he must pull this joke on people all day long. I took him up on his offer at the risk of being the fool of the joke.

I went over to the two poles as he instructed, cautious at first. It's no fun when everybody in the room knows you are about to get punked! As if the world were watching me, I thought I needed to muster all the strength I had just to move this thing. I figured, if I get it to move, the joke will be on them. HA!

I pulled.

It moved!

It moved forward just like he said. It took little effort on my part. It moved as easy as he said. And did I mention that all the people had boarded the carriage already? I moved it several inches with ease. I suppose I could have pulled it much farther than that. But his point was well made.

"Oh, I got it. The horse is for nostalgic purposes. This is just for show for the tourist," I said, as if I now I had seen the light.

"Well, not quite," he answered. "The horse does more than just look good for the people. The horse is the whole package."

Oh, here comes the punch line. I said, "I just pulled it."

And then he said something strange to me, "Yea, but you're not the whole package. You can pull it but…

you couldn't stop it."

Stop it?

I never thought about stopping it.

You see, once the inertia of all that weight begins moving forward, stopping it is where the real power is needed. Hardly anyone really comprehends or takes into account that not being able to stop something once you've started it is a concern.

I could get the carriage started. No problem.

But once I got it moving, how could I stop it?

The weight moving forward would be more than I could bear to handle on my own. "Your own strength would not have the power to stop what was so easy to start."

For the horse, all two thousand pounds of him would need to act. Every muscle in that horse would be called on to react to stop the carriage. What had begun moving forward is a tremendous amount of weight. Slowing it, and stopping it, couldn't be done with my power. No matter how simple it was to start.

As the horse was hooked and the tour of the city of Charleston began, the carriage went down an incline and out on the street. Halfway down and moving quickly, a car raced around the corner blowing the horn. The horse locked his front legs like a bodybuilder would flex in a competition. All the muscles snapped from front to back like a steel cable pulled tight.

The carriage stopped like it had disc brakes. All of us on the carriage shifted forward. Just then the driver looked around at me, his face grinning from ear to ear. "You see what I mean? You wouldn't have stopped it."

He was right. The consequences would have been devastating if the people would have depended on me to stop the carriage.

As the tour proceeded for the next several hours, I thought to myself,

This world is made up of things easy to start but hard to stop.

Do you have something in your life that you started and can't stop?

The newest credit card, eating the wrong foods, or just simply spending money. Perhaps it's something even more powerful than these. It has control of you. Are you looking for a way out and can't stop?

Sin has that same look and feel. You agree?

Psalm 9:16 reminds us that "the wicked are ensnared by the work of their hands."

It's easy for us to start something immoral, but we're wrong to think we can stop it at any time without the power of something greater. Like that two-thousand-pound horse, it takes a much higher power to stop what was so easy for me to start. Adam and Eve saw, pursued, acted on, and indulged in what God had forbidden. The rest is history.

Consequences come last and are thought about the least.

Many of us lean into situations that have lasting consequences. Being wooed by the latest trend. Being tempted by the world's ever growing call to seek dangerous ambitions for ourselves. All of that in the process of convincing ourselves that we are capable of stopping anytime we feel. It is a tragic combination.

Taking chances and leaning into what life has to offer is the way I like to live. I'm a dreamer, a risk-taker. But God figures into the equation each time, or I just shouldn't do it.

Knowing this, the next time you are enticed to start something that seems out of the character of God...

leave it alone!

Being able to stop it or not is the difference between a problem gone unchecked and proof that God is present in your life. Jesus is the filter through which we should sift everything…

every thought,

every action,

every consequence.

All our dreams are to be sifted this way.

Dreams are meant to chased. Many have been placed there by God. They inspire us. They add fuel to our souls, allowing us to live an extraordinary life. We are to lean forward and chase the wonders He has placed within our hearts, even when these dreams look like the weight of a carriage behind us. The litmus test? Ask this: Is God in the equation?

God designed us to seek and strive to do His will. But when those dreams and journeys morph into something else, trouble can gain speed. Stopping becomes physically impossible.

Let's be real. Here is an anonymous quote that best fits this scenario.

"When you sow a thought, you reap an act; when you sow an act, you reap conduct; when you sow conduct, you reap character; when you sow character, you reap a destiny."

The fun and the exciting part is always in the beginning, isn't it? Everything looks better in the beginning. Something new, something you've never tried before, something that's risky. We have the ability to get caught up in things that seem on the edge. We love pushing the envelope to the point of hyperventilation from sheer excitement. Cheating and getting away with it fuels us in the most diabolical way. People live for the thrill of a risk.

In modern terms they call these people thrill-seekers. Problem is

- sometimes people die doing it
- or become destroyed by it.

The governor from South Carolina had an affair with another woman. His wife and kids are the recipients of a husband and father gone astray. His life will never be the same. TV stations carried the confession live. All friends and family, co-workers, and fellow dignitaries are caught in the crossfire of feeling betrayed.

He had been involved with this woman for some time. He had been pulling this weight and the weight began to gain momentum. It started so easily and innocently. Eventually, he disappeared for days away from home and his family. The thought became an act. The act became a conduct in defiance. Now his destiny has been tarnished forever—who can trust him anymore? The lies are many.

All that weight is moving forward. It all started by a simple pull in the wrong direction.

One thing always leads to another when this situation happens.

The longer we stay pulling this weight around, the tougher it is to stop it. It gains momentum. A spiritual disintegration begins, and soon the smell of a rotting soul becomes evident to others, not just you.

Sin that goes unchecked is the road to destruction. Maybe not today or tomorrow, but it will come.

Do you fall into this category? Is there something that feels easy to pull along but you can't seem to stop it? Is the weight too great?

There are questions we should have asked at the beginning.

Why did this start?

How do we respond to situations like these when they present themselves?

How should we respond?

How we respond is the key.

We need to ask ourselves this question: If it was so easy to start, is it equally easy to stop?

If not, beware. The weight in the end may run right over the top of you.

SEEKING THE THIN PLACES...

1. When is the last time you began something that was easy to start and now you're unable to stop? Is it bad for you? If so, what's holding you back from quitting?

2. Is there a specific sin in your life that's gone unchecked? Does anyone know about it?

Entry #3

Where Is Everybody?

Conversation enriches the understanding,
but solitude is the school of genius.

—Edward Gibbon

Remember when you felt indestructible? A sense of no-one-can-do-it-better-than-you, whatever "it" may be.

Years ago I was teaching the "Kaleidoscope" class. It was named that because the people attending were from all parts of the world.

One was from Africa, one was from Asia, and the other was from Croatia.

That's all.

Did I forget to mention there were only three?

I taught every Wednesday night in the corner classroom of the church—the same church where I grew up. I was thrilled to be teaching.

Their English was spotty, at best. So, if I messed up and lost my place, I just acted as if I was pausing due to their lack of English. It was the perfect excuse when other pastors came to visit and listen in.

The class began right at 6:30 p.m. and went for about an hour. I had a blackboard and a lectern. I looked official. I prepped each week with a new Bible lesson. I studied and would sometimes bring in props to help with the lesson. I even brought in a world map to make everything look and seem authentic. I put it on the wall and referred to it maybe only once in five years, but it looked great!

It all started real innocently.

I was just following what my heart desired: to one day teach and maybe become a pastor. What a high calling of responsibility. This was great training ground to see if this thing would really take off and fly, if I was good enough. If my messages were well received. If people came to me and said how good they were, I must be on the right path. I looked forward to when the class would end so I could receive what people might say about me. That was a sure sign and litmus test that they were going to let me know how good I taught. If they praised me and told me it was great, I'd be in. But you know what, I've never heard anybody stay to tell you how bad you were, even if you were.

I couldn't lose.

It's amazing what you'll believe about yourself when people tell you what you want to hear.

As the class kept meeting, the class kept growing in numbers. Pretty soon, we needed more chairs. The number reached fifteen. My wife and son soon began to attend. I guess they had heard it wasn't all that bad. The more the class grew, the more I taught. The more I taught, the more I needed space to move around and become animated in my delivery. This was cool. I had all the plates spinning at one time.

Soon the class grew to almost thirty. Wow! Is this not great? Look at me. They're coming to hear the next guy. I wonder if word will get back to the senior pastor about this class. He may invite me to preach on a Sunday with all the success that I'm having. After all, it's about sharing and being a team, right? It's not about him.

I began inviting others to share what their country was about. I thought this would add some spice to the class. We even went out to local restaurants of their choosing just to try their native foods. It was a blast. Nothing could be better.

One Wednesday evening I arrived early to class to set up. My wife and son were not able to attend that night due to a scheduling conflict. No problem. *We'll still have thirty people, and this lesson tonight is the bomb. Wait till they hear this one*, I thought. As I prepared for the class, time got short. All would be coming soon. They normally arrived about ten minutes early so they could chat and catch up.

At twenty-five minutes after 6:00 p.m., nobody had arrived. Perhaps I had the wrong night. I had sent a reminder of what the lesson was going to be about. Well, 6:30 p.m. came and no one was there; perhaps a fire drill that I didn't hear. We had a big building, you know. A few minutes passed and still no one. I went from thirty people last week to not one person this week.

"Where is everybody?"

Nothing made sense. I was awesome in my teaching. I know because they told me. But now something was wrong, really wrong. But what I felt as being wrong was not the normal thought. I had the right day. I had the right room. I had the right lesson. I had me teaching it. Me! What more is there? As the room remained silent when normally it was bustling with voices by now, I sat in the chair and looked at the floor beneath me. I was distraught with feelings of rejection and pride all balled up into one heaping layer of self-centeredness. I looked for every excuse in the world why the class was not here. I mean all of them were absent. It would be different if there were somebody—but nobody?

When God wants to make a point, *He* sometimes unleashes the lesson designed for you in a hurtful but meaningful way right then in the moment.

This was one of those times.

There was a lesson for me in this—I just had to think about it for a moment. What I learned has impacted my being and my thinking since then.

As I sat there, I thought I had done all that God had asked me to do.

I was faithful in being there each Wednesday night.

I had not missed a class. I studied each week.

I made the best notes. Works and performance, right?

I dismissed the class right on time each week. So what was up?

As I sat in this empty room, my mind began to think. To think deeply. I reflected on all that I had done and accomplished for God.

Or was all this just to build me up with the call of God as an excuse?

Suddenly, my lesson had begun to reveal itself. Quickly. I was at a thin place. The mind has the ability to think at warp speed. It can retrace steps of the past, moving from stage to stage, within seconds. As the room remained quiet, the question was asked by God:

"Are you doing all this for yourself or for Me?"

I can count on one hand the number of times God has spoken to me directly. This is one of them. A very thin place where a question from God comes. My natural world and His supernatural world colliding.

I hesitated. That's the problem. If you hesitate to this question, look out. I pondered and waited, not wanting to answer but feeling that the answer had already been discovered. Was I promoting myself through my own ability? It's so easy to be consumed by one's own success. Oh, I know, you're thinking about the size of the class. What's to be admired? It's only a small class. Small is where most of the problems begin. Soon, small turns into something larger than what we can control.

What I've learned is many times we boost ourselves up out of jealousy. You take your eyes off God and start watching others do what they do. Soon, you become driven to surpass them.

I had witnessed others who had the incredible knack and giftedness of teaching and preaching. Why not me? I can do this. Maybe, but motivation is the key to everything. In all that we do, motivation is the starting gate. You exercise to either lose weight or stay in shape or both. You sit on the beach to either get a great tan or indulge in a great nap. You drink water because you're thirsty. The true motive is in the beginning of everything we do.

Think about it. Why do you do what you do? Right now. Are you working inside your giftedness, or are you maintaining and chasing a dream that's not meant for you? What motivation do you have to continue what you are presently doing?

I found out my motivation was all out of whack with reality and what God wanted me to be doing. I was proving something to me or someone else. Trying to prove constantly in life, hoping others will take notice and you will receive affirmation from them, is a dead-end street. You'll eventually arrive at a sign that may say:

> Original passions gone astray: TURN BACK!
> U-turns allowed: DO IT NOW!
> Find your passions—not the passions of others—and act: GO!
> Invest in others' lives; lose yours: HURRY!

Passions and motivations can become derailed in an instant. Just by watching others or perhaps hearing a comment about someone else can light the fuse of jealousy, which can turn into envy. This can lead to hatred if you are not careful.

King Saul was this type of person. Only hearing a comment about David drove Saul into a person who wanted to kill. In 1 Samuel 18, the story of Saul shows how Saul's jealousy motivated him to act. Saul was King. What else is there to prove? He's at the top of the food chain. But his eyes were watching David. "And David had success in all his undertakings; for the LORD was with him" (1 Sam. 18:14). What Saul had overheard was women singing, "Saul has slain his thousands, and David his ten thousands" (18:7).

Immediately Saul personalized this as a competition. Who is more superior? He felt challenged. Jealously raged within him, and his motivation took him down the road of destruction.

Well, let's go back to the room. My empty room. A room where I was ready to teach but no one was there to learn. As I sat there in this room, the quietness was deafening. The question God had asked was convicting.

I was doing for me. I was not being in Christ.

The more people who came to the class, the more I was convinced they came to hear me, not the message. That's a dead end.

Finally realizing the grave mistake I had made, I began to ask God for the forgiveness of my motivations and actions. I began the road back to where I should be going. All the signs pointed "This Way." Just as fast as God can hold you accountable and challenge you directly, *He* can restore you back to where you were meant to be as if nothing had happened.

The time was now twenty minutes until 7:00 p.m. Still no one.

Just then, the door opened and people began coming through. "Hey, brother, sorry we're late. We were all kept downstairs in the fellowship hall for an extra twenty minutes. A surprise speaker gave his testimony," one of the class regulars told me.

The entire class seemed to now be coming through the door. Within five minutes the room was full. Almost every chair was now taken and Bibles in hand. As the chatter filled the room and the excitement filled the place in expectation of studying God's Word, I began by telling them that I also had a surprise speaker. His message I will never forget.

I've wondered if I had not chosen the road of reflection and seeking forgiveness that night, would the guest speaker downstairs have spoken the entire time? It felt as if God would not have released them until I was willing to understand what was happening and change my motives.

After this night, I have tried to keep my word and calling as true as I possibly can. I am still vigilant to the trappings of the evil one. This night is seared into my memory as if it were yesterday. My Old Testament professor told me in class once, "You can sum up the entire Old Testament in one word: *remember*."

SEEKING THE THIN PLACES...

1. **Which gets the most attention with you?** The cheers or the jeers? Which one do you believe the most? Why?

2. **Lessons in life are sometimes painful.** Which lesson do you remember the most that still hurts?

3. **Have you ever felt betrayed by God?** What caused the feeling? Do you still feel this way?

Entry #4

The Bounty Hunter

But he, desiring to justify himself, said to Jesus,
"And who is my neighbor?"

—Luke 10:29

Who would have thought that the family weekend at the beach would take such a dramatic turn? I normally don't hear God's voice. I can count on one hand throughout my entire life how many times this has happened: twice, if you're keeping a box score. This scary weekend was one of those two.

It all started one Saturday morning. I went to the shower and this voice hit me, saying, "*You are going to have a flat tire today and Romans 8:28.*"

What?

Again, like an echo in a tunnel, the same voice and the same line spoke. I didn't tell my wife or son about this strange voice for fear of being laughed at. This was the day my family took our four-hour ride to the beach for the weekend. I could make that journey in my sleep. Nothing to fear. I knew the way by heart.

Have you ever driven roads so much that you don't even know what the names of the roads are?

People ask, "How do you get there?"

Ah... Not sure other than when the road turns into four lanes you're on the right track. But a flat tire and a Bible verse? What's up with that?

If they came to me in separate dreams, OK. It's not unusual to have a word come to you by a friend or perhaps a stranger that may make you reflect. But sensing two *possible* revelations that seemed so far apart made no sense.

Some things are just meant to be paired together: red meat and red wine, white wine and fish, pasta and meat sauce, and hamburgers and fries. But a flat tire and a Bible verse?

It was the dead of summer. We were traveling from Charlotte to all points on the South Carolina coast. The route we always take has us driving through Florence, South Carolina. We loaded the car early in the morning and off we went. No glitches. No strange happenings. Two hours into this trip, my wife and son with me, we were on a stretch of highway where there was nothing for miles.

What I have found out about God is anything God has you venturing into usually offers no logical meaning for us mere humans. Count on it. Logic goes right out the window.

Well, it began. Riding on a stretch of open road…

flap,

flap,

flap,

flap.

The tire! You've got to be kidding! I began to laugh. My wife and my son thought I had lost my mind. The left front tire was completely flat. Driving on the rim, I found the only place off the road I could go and still get level ground to put the car up on a jack. We all got out of the car on the side of this highway; it must have been close to one hundred degrees. Cars were passing by. If it had been dark, the fear factor would have been much higher.

My first thought? The inconvenience. Second thought? Some of my vacation time could end up being dribbled away sitting on the side of the road.

As I got out of the car to look at the damaged tire, a small car pulled in beside me. It was a car most adult men would have trouble fitting into. A man about 6'4" with blue jeans and a white, cut, tight T-shirt got out. He was an intimidating sight. Of course, anyone with a large magnum handgun on his belt in clear view would make anyone back up. My son and wife never came around to the other side of the car.

His actions indicated he was in a hurry. It seemed as if he was running from the local police. Maybe he had just robbed a bank down the road. His car was pulled in front of mine, and the only way I would be able to leave once the tire was fixed was in reverse. I had no AAA to call for assistance; this scary guy was my only option. Did he want my car as a getaway but just needed to fix it first?

"Seems like you got a flat," he said as he knelt down to examine the damage.

"Yea, it does appear that way."

"Well, grab the jack out of the trunk and let's see what we got," he responded.

It seemed rather funny and unusual that this guy was so willing to just jump in and help. Let's be frank; not many people just stop and take over a bad situation.

Normally, people go out of their way to not get involved. Sometimes people look the other way as if they didn't see your unfortunate predicament. Haven't you done that? I have. And then when something bad happens to you, you wonder why people seem not to care. They look right through you as if the person behind them will help you. Just not them.

I opened the trunk and took the jack out. He asked, "So, what do you do?"

"I'm a pastor," I said.

"Oh, well, I guess you are about as far away from what I do as it gets."

That made me nervous. "What do you do?"

As he answered, he stood up beside me and said, "I'm a bounty hunter."

"A what?"

He repeated himself. I somehow thought these people only existed on TV. "Yep, I just got back from Vegas handcuffing a runaway to the back seat while I drove three days back to the East Coast. He never woke up for those days, I made sure of it."

What the heck did that mean? I was afraid to ask.

"Your spare tire needs air too," he said. Without hesitation and looking at my son he barked out, "What do you say you send junior with me just down the road and I fill up the tire and be back in about fifteen minutes."

The vision I had running through my head was one of horror. I would never see my son again. And why was it necessary to send my son? As I shuffled my feet and began to feel nervous, I offered, "How about I go with you?"

"Not a problem," he said.

So, as I got in the car I realized that once in the car I couldn't get back out. There were no door handles from inside the car from which to escape. He really seemed to be a bounty hunter. I told my wife before I got in the car in a soft whisper that if I was not back in thirty minutes to call 911. I might already be dead. Serious! As the car pulled out, I saw the faces of my wife and son. It scared me because they had the expression that they might not see me again. That was not a comforting thought.

"What church do you attend?"

I told him I was from Charlotte and where I attended. He said he had lived in Florence all his life. He mentioned nothing about his family. In fact, he offered no information outside of that. After a couple miles down the road, we pulled into a gas station on the corner. We filled up the tire with air and off we went back to where my car and family were standing.

I finally had the courage to ask his name.

"I'm James," he said. He jumped out of the car and began to change my tire.

I must admit, even being a pastor and speaking in the past on the "Good Samaritan," I was somewhat skeptical of this encounter. It just didn't seem logical.

No one stops to help without a motive? Do they?

The tire was changed, but it was one of those tires that some people call "maypops." It may pop anytime.

As he finished putting the tire on the car, he spoke across the hood. "I tell you what you do. Go down about three miles and make a right at the light. Make sure you cross the railroad tracks as you make the turn. That way you'll know you on the right path. Then, go about six miles until you see an old, large oak tree on the left. Right behind the tree is a garage. Tell them James sent you; they'll know." He said good-bye and off he went.

I took all the directions down in my head. I pulled out on the highway and began to drive. I basically chalked this wild adventure up to being lucky. As I looked out the right window, James was next to my window. He was asking me to follow him. Movies I had seen in the past began to come to mind. You know the kind—the main characters in the story think they are rid of the danger and the danger keeps following them.

James had decided to take me where he had instructed. *I suppose I should follow,* I thought. *But is he really taking me to change my tire, or am I going to a place from which my family and I will never return?* I tried to keep a positive attitude. I thought for a moment, *At least I know now I won't get lost.* We took the right across the tracks as he said and went about six miles. Sure enough, the oak tree looked as if had been there since the Civil War. Right behind it was the tire place. It looked like something out of a Jackie Gleason / Burt Reynolds movie. I'm from the South, but I would have never stopped here to change a tire. Don't get me wrong; I love the South. But danger can be lurking anywhere anytime.

James pulled in ahead of me. He talked to one of the men inside. The only light that I could see inside was the light that the sun offered from the massive door being open all the way. This place was a throwback in time. As I got out of the car, James explained that my car was next. I thought that now was the time he would say good-bye and be on his way. I handed him some money for all his help and kindness.

Instead of leaving, he leaned up against my car and just looked off into the distance.

He wasn't leaving. Again, the movies replaced all the good thoughts in my head.

I was worried and apprehensive as to what he might now be wanting. "You know, I lived here all my life," he began. "My father was in Vietnam and has never been the same. My mother is always sick, and my life seems to always be in a mess."

I listened to him, trying to figure out how I might be able to best answer him. He had chosen to open up. Before, he said nothing. Now, he wanted to talk about everything. As I looked to the front of the tire place, underneath the oak tree, I never noticed the tire sign. Usually, signs promote the latest sales or advertisements. You know what was on the sign?

The only writing on the sign was a quote from the Bible: Romans 8:28.

That's it.

That's all that was on the sign!

It was hot as blue blazes that day, but I had more cold chills up my spine at that moment in time than I had ever had before.

Right then, God had me in this place for James.

I instantly remembered my morning shower. A flat tire and Romans 8:28. Only God can package these two things together that seem miles apart where they both come out in the end in harmony and for one cause.

Read the verse:

"We know that in everything God works for good with those who love him, who are called according to his purpose."

Divine appointments. God sometimes puts us into a position to help others without warning. The question is, would I have gone or trusted this path on my own? I could think of other ways to inspire me to help James. I wouldn't have chosen a flat tire, however. But through this experience, God let you learn about myself.

If you walk in pursuit of God, realizing that thin places can happen at any moment, be prepared for the challenge. You'll never see it coming. Be prepared to be tested. Be prepared to experience encounters that leave you shaking your head. The apostles walked in faith with little information but with great imagination.

Information has the ability to be discouraging.

Imagination has the ability to dream all things are possible.

This whole day made no sense until I arrived at the end. God sometimes shows us nothing until we're willing to go all the way and trust what He has planned for us.

But there is one lingering question, and it bothers me to this day. If the shoe had been on the other foot, would I have stopped for James?

Would I have stopped with him looking the way he did?

Would fear and unpredictability make me drive on?

In the parable of the Good Samaritan (Luke 10: 25-37), a priest and a Levite passed the man that needed help. Both of these men represented a higher calling. It was in their "job description" to stop and help. They would be in those days the most likely to see to the needs of this injured man.

But they didn't. They kept going. The least likely of people stopped. He was a Samaritan. Least likely because if you were a Samaritan, you were the one race that could not convert to Judaism. You could be a Greek or a Roman and could convert to Judaism. But not the Samaritan. Here was a man that was attending to a person that was most unlike him.

So, what we have is Jesus telling a story emphasizing that the least likely to stop and help stopped and helped. James on the road leading to the beach, not Jericho, stopped to help me. The individuals that should have stopped didn't. In Scripture, there are twelve things that the Samaritan did for this beaten man. James did the same for me. He stopped, took the tire off, drove to get it filled, took me to the place to get another tire, had the man put it on, saw that I was all right in the end, and made sure I knew my way back to the main road.

Today, I have lost touch with James. I invited him to church in the beginning of our encounter many times. Until now I wish I could say he took my offer. To my knowledge, he hasn't. I must remember, as we all should, that we just sow the seeds of the saving grace of Christ. Jesus waters it.

Who is our neighbor?

This I can tell you. James changed me in ways that I could have never imagined. Sometimes, in the thin places, God will test your character to see if it's authentic. The priest's and Levite's character and actions don't seem to match their talk. Authenticity took a hit. Transparency came to the forefront. It forced the priest and Levite to show their true nature.

What about yours?

Do you live two lives? One you proclaim to live and the one you really live outside viewing eyes? What I took away from this encounter with the bounty hunter is a reminder to live a life of consistency and upright character.

James presented a challenge to me without him knowing. Would I have stopped for him?

From that point on I am always aware for what might be next.

You never know when God will tell you: "Today, you will have a flat tire." Be ready!

SEEKING THE THIN PLACES...

1. Who have you helped that is least like you?

2. How do you define, "Who is my neighbor?"

3. Are you willing to follow God even when you can't see a thing?

Entry #5

The Gospel Is Like a Roller Coaster

Some were sick through their sinful ways, and because of their iniquities suffered affliction; they loathed any kind of food, and they drew near to the gates of death.

—Psalm 107:17-18

Do not love the world or the things in the world. If anyone loves the world, love for the Father is not in him.

—1 John 2:15

ave you ever been on a roller coaster that changed your life? During the ride, did the thought occur to you that you may not survive it? Or that if you did make it, you promised God in the process a list of things never to do again?

It's been my experience that the name of some of these coasters are designed to change your mind while waiting in line. "The Loch Ness Monster." "The

Mindbender." "The Big Bad Wolf." I mean, come on! They put the most horrific part of the ride directly in front of you where you're waiting your turn. That will get your emotions churning if nothing else will.

The bad thing for me is if I get too excited, scared or not, I need to find the restroom. Sorry, TMI. I remember the last time I was on one of these rides. It was thrilling. You raise your hands as the tracks turn a 360-degree loop, all the while hoping this thing doesn't stop in the wrong place.

As the coaster pulled into the station to let us all off, I wasn't feeling well. I had grown older; some things on the body don't act the same anymore. I had acquired an inner ear disorder called vertigo. The older I get, the more severe it has become. It's motion sickness of the worse kind. It takes hours, sometimes days to go away. Unless I have medication right away, I could be in for a long, agonizing time.

In my last year in seminary, one of my professors told a story about his family being on vacation. He and his wife and children went to the amusement park one day. As the gates opened, the kids made a straight line for, of course, the roller coaster. The line was already filling up quickly. He went with the kids and took a seat on the bench outside the rails that formed the line. "Come on, Dad!" they yelled. "Ride with us." He told us as he sat there he pleaded with them to just let him watch. They persisted and begged him to ride.

Finally, he gave in and decided to ride. It was a coaster that turns you in all directions. Upside down. Hairpin turns. Dark tunnels to go through where you can't see a thing. And then, down one of the steepest hills around—while dropping at speeds only designed for highway driving.

He told us little about the ride itself. The only thing we had to go on was that once the ride was over he stumbled to the park bench. The word *stumbled* was explanation enough. He had gotten motion sick on a ride he never wanted to be on. No matter how long he sat there and watched others, the feeling of being sick stayed with him. It was a long day.

The kids? They raced to get back in line. They wanted the thrill of the experience again. This time they knew in some way what the ride was like, and they loved it. They couldn't get enough hairpin turns, dark shooting tunnels, steep hills that challenged Isaac Newton's theory of gravity, and loops that left you with empty pockets because all your coins were falling to the ground.

And then he said, "You know, class, Christianity is like a roller coaster."

The room fell quiet.

"Some people see Christianity as a life that they cannot be a part of. It gives them motion sickness."

His words made sense. A roller coaster can seem intimidating, scary. It has turns and dark tunnels where it is impossible to see what lies ahead.

The person who refuses to ride? The person who rides and sits on the park bench after the fact? They take the position: "It's not for me." No matter how much you beg them to take this incredible journey of twists and turns that seemingly defies death, they refuse.

The coaster represents a radical change from everything else in the park. For the most part, the rest of the rides seem tamed and straightforward. But to refuse the ride—the journey of a lifetime—is to say I have better options, I have ideas that surpass this ride, the Jesus revolution is not for me.

Christ desires to take us on the most thrilling ride of life. It's where what we think we need and what God has for us meet in the intersection with startling impact.

For some, experiencing the life of a Jesus follower is not appealing. They hear the screams of excitement. They see the people in line who wait for hours to ride a ride that takes less than three minutes. They stand on the sidelines in a self-consuming world and insist beyond understanding that the thrill of riding this amazing ride called "The Jesus Follower" is not for them. They would rather be in a world consisting of circumstances that they can control.

To experience a thin place, we need to be at a place where God is in total control. He impacts us so we can experience the maximum benefit from what He is doing.

Moses was on the mountaintop for the thrill ride of a lifetime that he could never imagine on his own.

David ventured down into the valley to punch a ticket on this ride that allowed God to manifest His power and defeat the giant. Without God, David would have never walked down to face the giant with the simple weapon he had in his hand.

Imagine interviewing Moses and David after the fact.

What would they have said?

What would they have changed?

Nothing! Did they know ahead of time what the experience was going to be like? Nope. Not even close. You couldn't make up a story like these two stories. David had witnesses; Moses had no witnesses.

At least people saw what David did through the eyes and power of God. Moses, on the other hand, spent some time convincing the people of his encounter. I've done that with a coaster in the past. Rode the most awesome ride known to man and my friends didn't believe me when I got home. Was I scared? You betcha! Out of my wits! But say this is the true definition of *courage*: "Scared to death but you do it anyway." That about sums it up.

For David and Moses, it took courage. They got on despite the shrieking noise and the death-defying speeds. Jesus never said it would be a ride in comfort; He never said it would be a ride of complacency. You get on the "Jesus Follower" and you are in for a thin place where God acts and you receive. And hang on.

Peter, James, and John made a decision to punch a ticket after fishing all night and decided to ride the "Jesus Follower." Nowhere in the account of this calling do you read questions that I would have certainly asked before I cleared the backyard and hung up my fishing pole:

When are we coming back?

Where are we sleeping?

What happens to the business while I'm gone?

How much money are we going to make?

How far are we walking?

Are we the only three going?

Anybody ever get sick on this journey?

When do we eat?

I've asked some of the same probing questions while in line for the coaster.

How long is the ride?

What's the worst part?

How fast does it go and how high is the hill?

Have you ever gotten sick on this thing?

I may have to skip lunch after this ride.

Coaster riders, they live for the adventure. They travel miles to ride the best, fastest, scariest, most heart-wrenching ride in the country. They can't get enough. Which takes me back to the kids in line.

These kids in this story represent the kind of follower Jesus is looking for. Fearless. Risk-taking. Confident. Not scared of failure. Above all, a person who runs to the line again no matter what comes their way and rides the "Jesus Follower" again and again.

What about you? Have you ever shied away from the risk of seeking God and desired what the world had to offer you? If so, you're the one on the bench in the park. Comfortable. Secure. No risk. Content to sit and observe, having never engaged life to the fullest.

Have you ever trusted Christ with your life and rode the most thrilling ride of your life?

Have you ever seized the moment and know that it changed your life forever?

Or did you miss it?

Not punch your ticket and pass up the journey of a lifetime?

You still have time. Don't let anyone tell you different.

My advice? The next time you see a roller coaster, look at it through a different set of eyes. God is calling you to something greater than yourself—something exciting, something that leads through turns pulling six g's, and then shooting a tunnel not knowing where the other side is.

If you're not careful, riding the "Jesus Follower" may be just for you.

You may find yourself running back to get in line again and again and again.

SEEKING THE THIN PLACES...

1. **What is the worst ride you've ever been on?** Did you ride again?

2. **Are there parts of following Jesus that make you motion sick?**

3. **How much does control of your life get in the way of following God?**

Preach to Three Like a Thousand

My soul, wait thou only upon God;
for my expectation is from him.

—Psalm 62:5 *KJV*

W hen I was a pastor on staff at a church, we had the opportunity to serve an outreach ministry to military troops. This was in the days of the Iraq War. I met Major Chaplin Watters at the church one day during a conference. We began a conversation that is still going today. In fact, we have become close friends even though he now has moved on to the Pentagon.

We thought it would be really cool to make a trip to Fort Bragg in eastern North Carolina and speak to the troops. I was warned in the beginning that troops are sometimes tough to reach.

Over the course of six months, I began to put a team together for the trip. I was trying to put the best people on the ground that could connect with the soldiers in a simple but profound way.

As the time approached to go, "Chappy"—as I have always called him—told me to expect some seven hundred to one thousand troops for this ministry outreach. It was going to be great. We had several bands. We had a video playing. We had a comedian come along. And we'd planned a great speaker who once played professional sports.

It was all coming together. Expectations were high. The facility was set. Everybody was excited. Everybody knew what their duties and responsibilities were. All we needed now was the clock to hit the mark and the curtain to go up. All would be blessed by a great performance and a great message.

Funny thing. The clock hit the mark and everyone was in their places, the curtain went up and…

not one person showed up.

Seven hundred to one thousand troops expected to be here and…

no one!

Did we have the wrong day? What was going on?

Have you ever planned something that took weeks, perhaps months to prepare and it all fell on its face? It was as if we were expecting the Sermon on the Mount and all we got was a large empty room.

Did you ever go ahead of God?

Your plans, your kingdom values, your strategic initiatives, and your global worldview. Sometimes, in all our planning, what God has for us gets lost in the shuffle. We tend to do things that match what we can do comfortably and on our schedule.

God in the thin places *never* cooperates the way we want Him to cooperate. Never. Think about it. If He did, why would we need Him? God acts on our behalf to change things, reverse things, carry out things that otherwise we would not venture to do ourselves. We had planned for this day for God to be glorified, and it all went *crash*! What set in was…

frustration

anger

bewilderment

failure.

Let me ask you again. Have you ever felt like God let you down? I stood in the back of the theater at a loss for words. What I learned on this day is that to enter into a thin place with God is to enter with no premonitions of what may happen. To understand it's not about us. It's not about what we can accomplish—even in God's name. It's about Christ and what *He* has for us. To us, one thousand people would make the day a success. It makes the entire trip a success.

It's all about numbers. Right? That's what the world would have us believe.

Church growth. Everybody wants numbers to be high because it's a direct reflection of where the church is going: up. But on this day, God had something else in mind. Numbers played the least significant role in the whole adventure.

I can't help but ask a question that I feel all leaders in ministry perhaps need to ask of themselves: Could we be doing ministry each day and getting so caught up in the "doing" that we are forgetting the "being" in Christ?

Is it possible that as leaders of the church we could walk and talk with Christ day to day and totally miss *His* calling on our lives and who *He* really is?

Back to that day. Our team was very disappointed. Eventually, close to fifteen troops showed up and had an incredible experience. How do I know? They told me on the way out. It was a blessing to them just to be there.

It's not hard to miss the central theme of Scripture. Jesus said when we're loving the least of these, we're loving Him.

Numbers are insignificant.

Change the world one at a time.

But how? How can we do this with the right perspective and motive?

Light a candle; it has the ability to light up an entire stadium. And the greater the darkness, the brighter even a small flame will appear. What I needed to realize was I was not here to build an organization of followers but a kingdom of believers one at a time for all eternity.

A thin place on this day was about investment in the few. God made that clear. Small numbers. When we, as a church body, are willing to forgo size and expansion in exchange for treating one like our neighbor—a person who looks and acts nothing like us—then something special happens. God acts in a mighty way. That's why the story of the Good Samaritan gets so much attention. It's about serving the least and the lost one at a time—or, in this case, fifteen at a time. The truth of the matter is that we were expecting a catastrophic event happening in the lives of hundreds. God said nope. Invest in these and I will be glorified. Last time I looked, Jesus invested in the lives of twelve people, no more. Numbers…I don't think so.

People know sincerity and genuine love when they see it. These troops felt embraced and cared for, if for only a brief period of time. They saw a group of people who perhaps were nothing like them. Yet they felt loved. They felt a God that truly cared for them and was present in their lives.

A thin place is where the supernatural and natural world collide. A place where our soul needs to wait on God and witness up close *His* mighty works.

SEEKING THE THIN PLACES...

1. **Do numbers dictate success for you?**

2. **Are you reluctant to engage others who look, act, and dress nothing like you?** If so, why is this so hard?

3. **What scenario did God take and turn into a positive that seemed doomed from the beginning?**

Entry #7

Three Things
I Needed

Man's chief merit consists in resisting the impulses of his nature.

—Samuel Johnson

We live in a world that convinces us that to acquire something we have the ability to get it—whatever "it" is. We humans have a sense of destiny driven by our own abilities saying to us that we are the final say.

Carpe Diem!

Manifest Destiny!

It's all about human ingenuity and the power of the mind to achieve. Even in the worst of circumstances, we need to pull ourselves up by the bootstraps, dig in, and really see what we are made of. That's the American way. That's the world's way. Voices echoing all over the corridors of our intellect saying, *Listen to your innermost thoughts; the* secret *lies within you.*

Leighton Ford perhaps said it best and most simply in his book *The Attentive Life*: "In the Moses-Pharaoh encounter I hear the lifelong struggle in my own soul between God's voice and all the others."[1]

That is exactly what it is—a struggle between two competing voices. Both desire to be the captain of your ship. God desires to be the first and final answer to all our needs and problems. When that does not happen, He gets pushed down to some other classification of "call you when I need you."

While my son was graduating high school and was months away from going to college, life for my wife and me was upside down. I had recently lost my mother to a debilitating disease. I had no job to speak of. Out of work meant no income. Owing property taxes. And a son desiring to go to college.

Three things I needed.

I needed a job, which would lead to the ability to pay the taxes on the house and a way to pay for my son's college. These three things I needed to be taken care of fast.

As one of the afternoons slipped into evening, the doorbell rang. My son was home from school and answered the door. A sheriff stood at the door with a folder tightly sealed. As I approached the sheriff, he began to tell me of the problem. My son looked on and heard every word that was spoken. To this day, my son's question to me still hurts deep inside.

I was just informed by the law that if the taxes on my house were not paid within the next ninety days, my house would be foreclosed on. Gone. No house, no place to go, no job, no school for my son. A dead-end street in all directions.

---

1   Ford, *The Attentive Life*, 59.

I was shocked to find myself in such a bad way so fast. It all came crashing down at once. The world says you have the answers within you, yet it is the world that will crush you and betray you if you can't find it. Live by the sword, die by the sword. My father use to tell me, "It's a dog-eat-dog world, and I got Milk-Bone® underwear." I get that now.

Oh yes, my son's question: "Dad, are they going to take our house?"

His face told it all. He was worried. He was fearful. His one and only security blanket to shield the outside world might be disappearing within three months. I had no answer for him. I wanted to say, "No, they won't take our home." But the reality was they would if I couldn't find a way to get the taxes paid. To do that I needed a job, any job. And I needed to get my son in college.

My house was at stake.

My son's school was at stake.

My taxes being paid were at stake.

They say you can count on two things in life: paying taxes and dying. I wished for the second option. It seemed to be an easier path.

As I began to work the phone lines of all the people I knew who could maybe help me, no one could help. I knew a lot of people in this town; I grew up here. If anyone could find a way, I could. I leveraged every relationship I had. I called bank after bank looking for a loan. Nothing.

I called about jobs, nothing. I called again to friends and relatives. Nothing. It's amazing how people disappear from your sight when things get rough.

Have you ever experienced that in your life?

People you thought you knew, you didn't know?

You ever feel all alone?

No one to care? No one to even share your deepest-felt despair with?

This is the world sometimes. It builds you up, and if things go wrong, it tears you down. The world and the people abandon you in the greatest of moments. I had no one else to call out of my Rolodex™. I was down to the letter *Z*, and my options were running out rapidly.

I could actually envision the sheriff coming back to my house as my son looked on to watch a sign be posted in my yard. Can you imagine that? The one thing I had left to offer for security for him and my wife was going away.

I have never had such a sick feeling of failure and loneliness consume me in all of my life. As several days went by, I sat in a chair silently. Done! Life was killing me, opportunities and dreams of living a life of prosperity vanishing like the morning dew.

Until my wife asked me a direct question.

She had been mostly silent all this time, letting me run things. I was making all the decisions and getting deeper in a hole. She respected my attempt to be the man of the house. All major decisions she delegated over to me. That was her role, right? She is the helpmate. But her question was filled with faith and an understanding of who really is in charge.

"Have you ever asked God for help? Have you ever asked God what you should do?" she asked. The room fell silent—silent from the realization that I had never considered it, and I was embarrassed to admit I hadn't.

Have you ever been hit by reality so bad you were speechless? My gosh, I was a person who was in seminary and studying to be a messenger for Christ.

I had asked everybody for help, except God.

Do you really feel God can help you quicker than someone you physically know and can see? Do you really feel God in His quiet and subtle way can come through for you in your deepest and darkest hour?

Are you just pretending that your faith will carry you through, while all along you know it won't? God will test the most hardened of faithful. Jesus asked Philip before feeding the multitude a quick and direct question. "How are we to buy bread, so that these people may eat?" Jesus said this to test him. Jesus knew the answer. The question was simply a way of asking Philip, "Is your faith indeed truly real?"

Do you believe in Me? Do you have the faith that I am here always?

That was my wife's question to me. That was God's question to me. That is my question for us all. Is your faith real, or are you just window dressing for everyone else to see? Has God quickly tested you? How did you respond? In faith, or did you seek answers from somewhere else?

In Christ, are we living a life of conquest or a life of compromise?

Are we running to the battle lines like David, or has our faith paralyzed us into apathy? Apathy can also take the shape of seeking answers that are not of God, and so we compromise. Compromise can be non-action. Just ask David's brothers, standing on the hill, looking at the giant, and convincing themselves it was a mountain they couldn't move.

"For truly, I say to you, if you have faith as a grain of mustard seed, you will say to this mountain, 'Move from here to there,' and it will move; and nothing will be impossible to you" (Matt. 17:20).

I must admit that my wife's question was right on the mark. But, even though I knew she was right, I hesitated. I paused as if I questioned God. Could He really pull this off for me? Did He really know what was at stake?

I could lose my house!

What happens if He takes too long to answer? Now what? My wife stared me down into a posture of kneeling and praying. As much as I prayed to have all three problems solved, my mustard seed faith was not even visible on the Holy radar screen. I prayed with doubt. Sound familiar?

You can preach and teach this prayer thing all day long. Do you really believe Him when you're the one at stake?

I finished my half-hearted prayer. I could just feel God hearing me cry out, and yet my faith was missing. I felt as if God was just looking at me, shaking His head and saying, *"Another one following Me and proclaiming My love and power, and yet he questions."*

Several days went by. I heard nothing. All was quiet, and the time was ticking. Anxiety had set in at a torrid pace. Fear was now a reality I could no longer hide. What was I to do? It was one of the darkest hours of my life. I could not help myself. Would I admit that God was in place to do some incredible things?

As another afternoon was melting away, the phone rang. I answered it, and on the other line was a woman's voice. She asked if she had the right person. I said yes. She proceeded to tell me that she was a lender of a bank and was calling me for some financial information. I paused, thinking that this was a bank I had never contacted. How did this bank know to call me, and who gave her my number?

My financial information was terrible. My credit scores were too low to be considered. To me, this was just another formality leading to a typical response: "Sorry, we can't help you at this time."

The more I answered her pointed questions, the more she seemed to reflect through her voice that things were looking up. I'm not sure how because when you are as low as I was, you can't see the surface at all. The call ended with the promise she would call back within a one-day period either lending me the money I needed or not. Skeptical, I hung up the phone and knew that the call tomorrow would yield another rejection.

Right before the banks closed at five o'clock, the phone rang. The same day, just two hours later.

The same lady was calling from the bank. I knew when I answered that this was typical of banks not to waste time if they already knew the answer. I knew what the answer would be; after all, it wouldn't take long to check and know I had very little to offer. As I awaited the predictable answer, she began.

"Sir, I have decided to take the risk and loan you what you need. I know the numbers don't add up on paper, but for some uncanny and illogical reason I feel this is a loan we can live with."

God is never about logic.

God is never predictable.

Is it possible that God wants to do the most incredible thing in our lives and in our community as believers that in some sense we would settle for less if not for His power of possibilities showing us there is something greater?

Quite simply, I felt God could not do something this big. I had put limits on God. I had God in a box. God had parameters and edges. God was predictable.

Now what? I didn't know how to react. Was this really happening? I shared the news with my wife. She took the news in stride as if to say, "What did you expect?"

Do we pray with the idea of expecting in return God's answer?

As the sun rose the next day, I had some hope of survival. I could possibly now pay my taxes, but how would I pay that loan back? Is that not like us to have God answer a prayer, and instead of praising God, we find another question to be concerned over?

Has doubt caused you to miss what God desired to do in your life?

How many of us choose a life far less and safe instead of encountering the extraordinary life God has planned we would live if we just trusted Him?

The phone rang again. It was a gentlemen I had

never spoken to,

never heard of,

was not aware of the job position he was proposing at one of the local churches,

never contacted.

How did he get my name and number? He said he had run into a person who knew me and thought he should give me a call. And now he was calling. The position was a ministerial position that I would have done for free but under the current circumstances I needed the money. He asked if I would be available for an interview.

Even through God's providence, He still asks if we are interested.

Two phone calls I had never predicted. I did not know either party—not the bank, not the church.

In the meantime, my son was asking if I could take him to the college of his choice. It was a great school with a great reputation for academics. The tuition was off the chart. I didn't want to take him. His grades were suspect; the disappointment for him would be more than I could stand. My wife said, "Take him and let him see the school." Somehow her faith in all things kept pushing and challenging me. It made no logical sense.

Meeting with an admissions officer, my son's opportunities were endless. My son loved the school. Exactly what I was afraid of; love it and then find out there is no chance of getting in. As we began to leave, the admin person said he should choose to go to the school full-time. The reason for her comment was that I suggested he could never get in under being a full matriculated student. I was persuaded after some time to agree to the chances of him being accepted full-time. I left full of doubt, already rehearsing my speech once he was turned down.

Whatever the school's decision was, it would need to be made quickly. Classes began in two days. No chance! What would I say to counterbalance his rejection from the school?

The next two days unfolded, and I went to the interview. A pastor interviewed me for several hours. Before I left that day, the job was mine. Can't explain it. I left with a job that I had never contacted this man for. Crazy thing about this position—they wanted me to begin the very next day. Serious? Yep.

As the bank was calling me in my new office the next day, working on all the loan papers, I received the dreaded call from the school. I had a job and loan money to save my home. Now the school. As the admissions officer spoke to me, the next few minutes changed my faith dramatically for the rest of my life.

"Mr. Furr, our school has decided to accept your son full-time into the program as an incoming freshman. He will need to report right away for his assignments and his books," she said.

What?

What?

You're kidding me?

He's in the school?

My son?

His grades were not that good. Are you sure?

As you can tell, my doubt runneth over. Instantly, what do you think I was now thinking? Did you guess it?

MONEY!

How was I going to pay for this school? You ever miss God's blessing completely? You were blessed and you missed it? He got in the college of his choice, and I was worried about the tuition. Human nature seems to focus on the mountain to climb instead of taking in the plateaus God lets us enjoy on the way up.

I had to ask the obvious question: "Where do I begin to fill out the loan papers? I mean, that's great he got in, but who do I see about loaning money? I've never been through this process before."

A voice answered me as if I had not heard everything.

"Well, that's the other thing I want to talk to you about." She said, "You see, Mr. Furr, our academic advisors have been looking at the classes your son took in high school. They have qualified him for several grants."

I paused for the moment. What was she really saying? "Do you mean he has access to some free tuition money?" was my response.

"Well, yes." She seemed to hesitate.

"Spell it out for me, please." Here was the faith change in me.

"You see, Mr. Furr, your son has taken classes that qualify him for grants, and because he was admitted late to the school, we have available leftover grants for his use. What I mean is...

"We are offering your son a full ride to come to the school. You owe us no tuition. His schooling is free."

I cried on the phone. Period.

God not only answered my prayers, but He went one more. God put my son in school, but He also paid for it. It happened this way because he was a late admittance to the school. If he had applied early, chances are the grants would not have been there for him to use.

All I could focus on sitting in my new office was that after all my calling, talking to people for help, desperately searching for a human answer to these three things I needed, God then showed me that He is the first option—always. Not second, not third. First.

I had a new job.

I had a new loan through the bank.

I had a school for my son that was paid for.

All in God's timing.

The next time you feel the world has you by the throat, life is closing in, you start searching your memory for connections that could possibly help you…

…remember your first option.

I encountered God in a thin place that only He could go to. No other people had the ability to come through for me. Powerful people mean nothing to God.

Only God has the power and answers you need.

SEEKING THE THIN PLACES...

1. **Have you ever been at the end of your rope in life and only God could help you?** Did you even call on Him? Why or why not?

2. **Is God always the first option, the only option, for you when making decisions?** Why or why not?

3. **Are you too prideful to ask God for help?** How much of your decisions are based on your own ability to make it happen?

Entry #8

God Has
the Final Word

Our thoughts create our reality—where we put our focus is the direction we tend to go.

—Peter McWilliams

I have led mission teams all over the world. What I can tell you is that something will go wrong no matter how much you plan. What you need to plan on is something going differently than intended. My focus has largely been to encourage and equip the locals in whatever country we visit.

As Americans we think like this. We are participating in missions so we are there for them. It's all about the mission. The church, as Erwin McManus says, exists for missions. He is right. But missions has a way of leading to moments that are unforgettable and sustain us for a lifetime.

Focus on giving,

focus on equipping.

focus on encouraging,

and then let God water the seed we desire to plant in others.

Several years ago I led a team of twenty-one people to Belgium. The team was larger than I usually led. But on this trip, we had multiple outreaches being worked on at the same time. On the flight over, we had a long stop in Atlanta. I mean, *long*—almost six hours. With a team that large, sitting in one spot gets crowded. So I decided to make an executive decision.

"Why don't all of you walk around the airport for several hours and be back at a certain time for boarding? I'll watch all the luggage." They took to that like bees on honey. Luggage was flying everywhere. I stayed for one main reason, and that was to put the finishing touches on a message to be delivered on Sunday. If they were all gone, I had my complete attention and I could concentrate the way I wanted to.

They all went their separate ways and disappeared into the crowded terminal. I focused on the message and began to handwrite some of the changes needed in the spaces. Airports are usually loud and bustling with excitement. For some reason, near my exit gate hardly anyone was around. I seemed to be by myself.

Weird.

But then through the quietness a voice rang sharply in my head.

"This mission trip is not for the people you are intending to reach. This trip is about someone on your team. The focus is not the target you intended. The focus is someone traveling with you."

I looked up, thinking someone was standing there; I was alone. The voice had come and gone. It was as if I had a conversation with someone, but in this large terminal no one other than me was at the gate. I have said before that God never talks directly to me. It always comes through other people and venues. Here I go again.

A thin place where God communicates His purpose and intentions. How was I to know whom God had targeted? I had twenty-one on the team.

One thing I have learned: keep your spiritual eyes and head on a swivel. Many times God focuses on someone not in the center of the picture.

Seriously, who would have chosen Moses?

Who would have been "all-in" in favor of Esther to speak to a king and risk the lives of an entire nation?

Superpowers all around, and some little known man walking through the desert is picked to be the father of a nation by God—

Abraham? Really?

And, after reading about the apostle Paul's life, I would have let him perish like the rest of the enemies of the gospel. But no! God chooses to make him the greatest missionary that the world has ever seen.

Goliath? You know he never anticipated some kid from the back of the ranks used by God to move onto the battlefield and claim victory for the nation of Israel.

Who was this person? Would I ever find out? As the team slowly returned over time, we boarded the plane for the overnight flight. On location, our accommodations were rustic. We all shared rooms outside of Brussels in a small town known for its mussels in white wine sauce. However, we cooked inside for most of the meals on this nine-day journey.

Each day our team split into two groups. In the evening we all came together in the library for an evening devotion. I chose different team members to lead each night. They had the freedom to do what they wanted—

read a devotion,

personalize the time,

question and answers.

It wasn't until the last night that the person God was focusing on was revealed. I was shocked to learn which of the twenty-one team members God had picked to reveal Himself to in a most dynamic way. Out of twenty-one people, I would have chosen this person last on the list. Goes to show you what I know about God's thinking.

The final night was the highlight of the trip. The team talked about their lives. They exposed personal things to the rest of the group that had never been known before. What was amazing is that the person whom God had chosen was the child of our senior pastor. Everyone thought she had it all together. Life was great and at her fingertips. She was smart, ambitious, pretty, outgoing, with friends from all directions and a desire to try life on her own. She was living a life of high expectations that others put on her, mostly her own family, her own dad.

You ever try to live up to someone else's desire for your life?

Are you living a life molded by the past?

Are you fighting against a ghost that you can never convince you are worthy just by being who you are?

Trying to fulfill what others have planned for you is a dead-end road.

She opened up in a way only God could have revealed. Others around her on the team made her see that a life built on her dreams and visions is a life lived to the fullest. Now, years later, I think of that night and how it had the ability to transform her way of seeking God's desire for her—not her father's.

Even though he is a pastor, he is human. God is head of the church, and when He leads beside the still waters and all seems lonely, He will restore the soul into a life that flourishes and a life that blesses others.

God has the final word.

Will we listen? Will we receive?

SEEKING THE THIN PLACES...

1. **Have you ever been surprised by what God did in your life?** Did you see it coming?

2. **Has God chosen you for some task and you feel inadequate?** Perhaps you're too confident. Is there a lesson you need to learn before God can use you?

3. **Do you listen to God easily?** What needs to change if not?

Entry #9

Stranger on a Plane

Sometimes it takes a little pain to get us to do the right thing.

—Rob Bell, *Jesus Wants to Save Christians*

We Christians can get comfortable. Would you agree? It's so easy to sit back and minister to the flock that knows us best. Jesus says,

I am the good shepherd; I know my own and my own know me, as the Father knows me and I know the Father; and I lay down my life for the sheep. And I have other sheep, that are not of this fold; I must bring them also, and they heed my voice. (John 10:14-16)

The problem comes when we meet people we don't know and God wants us to minister to them. You have no starting point, no point of reference. You know nothing about them.

As long as we stay in our own sheep pen, things seem normal. Even when it's not for us shepherds. We know these folks. People we talk to and have coffee with. We see them each week at the next service. Familiarity is a safeguard. It's a comfort zone. That's what makes the calling of the first disciples so amazing. They left what they knew and walked into a future that they knew nothing about. They were going to encounter people that were perhaps opposite of their values.

Engaging people not like us is pressure for most of us.

Years ago I had to struggle through a sickness with a brother-in-law. He had cancer all over his body; he was forty years old. I feel it is safe to say of my five brothers-in-law at that time that he was my favorite. My other brothers-in law would say the same thing about Jeff. He was their favorite too. He had this life about him that when you were around him he elevated life to a whole other level. He was also the funniest person I have ever met.

I was in Atlanta visiting my sister when I received a phone call. "You better come quickly; his time is very short." I scrambled to drive back home—four hours away. I flew to New York later the next day.

He was bad. The cancer had taken most of him already and time was slipping away.

Jeff passed away the next afternoon. Watching him take his last breath was troubling for me. I had lost a dear friend for the rest of my life. I went outside into the yard to make some calls to others who knew him.

I attended the funeral and then left for home, flying from New York to Atlanta.

The entire flight I asked God lots of questions. Most desperately out of all the questions, I asked God to minister to me. I was hurting, I had lost my friend. In my greatest time of need, I felt God owed a visit to me. You ever feel that way? You encounter tragedy and somehow you reason that God was at fault and now He owes you? After all, God got me into this relationship and now Jeff is gone. "I need You to explain that to me," I said. But, just like God, the one thing you desire to have He turns upside down. I wished for a word of encouragement, a word of "It's going to be OK."

It never came.

As I boarded the plane in Atlanta for the short flight home, my wife and I sat quietly. Looking forward. How do we process such great loss? What will we do at the next family sit-down? "Hey, God! Where are You?" As the plane filled to capacity, the seat beside me on the aisle was empty. The last gentlemen to board took the seat.

He was quiet,

he seemed troubled,

he seemed preoccupied in thought,

he seemed worried.

I struggled to get out a word to him to say hello. Finally, I introduced myself. He was around thirty-five years old. We exchanged hellos and the plane left the ground. Several minutes into this forty-minute flight, he asked if I was going home. "Yes, I am," I replied. I wanted so much to tell him of my recent grief. Perhaps he would be a great listening ear for me. This perhaps was the person God had sent to me. Now I could unload my personal feelings on the guy God had sent.

And then he began to talk. He said he was going home to see his mother. He had not seen her in a long time. Again, he looked as if he didn't want to be on this plane. I asked him about his mom. I completely forgot what I was dealing with.

"How old is she, and how long has it been since you moved away?" I asked. He had just moved the year before, but now he was coming to see her under some difficult circumstances. "What is the problem?"

"My mother has Alzheimer's. She doesn't know me anymore." The tears came to his cheek. This was a grown man crying on the plane. But he had a mother he loved greatly, and he was the only child. I felt sadness and pain for him. I felt he was drowning in lack of understanding of where this tragic road may lead. And then he asked me a question I will not forget.

"Would you know anything about Alzheimer's?"

The question seems benign. What's the big deal with that question? God has a special way of doing things. He turns your expectations upside down. Instead of me receiving encouragement, God asked me to give it away.

The old adage says, "The best way to eliminate self-pity or focusing too much on your problems is to go and help someone else with theirs." I never could understand that. In fact, I would say that it doesn't work. It's contrary to logic.

I'm hurting, so I need to go help someone else?

The first thing out of my mouth was, "It's going to be OK." *How can I say this? What I didn't tell you is my mother died of Alzheimer's. I was her only caregiver. I walked this disease with my mom for years. It was hard and exhausting. It was frustrating; it seemed at times it could not get any worse. I had very little help in dealing with this sickness. The one thing I always wished for was a person that knew the disease up close and personal. A person that could give me facts, not opinions, about what I was facing in the road ahead.*

Out of my pain I was able to help someone else.

Loss of a loved one and the pain I felt put me in a place to minister to someone else in their pain. Would I have been in this situation if not for my loss? Most likely not. I'm not about to tell you that the death of Jeff and the reason behind it led to a meeting with a stranger on a plane. But God has a way of putting us with people who need to hear an encouraging word out of pain we could never imagine.

Have you been in this situation?

Have you been so covered up in your pain that others were invisible to you?

In your trials of life, have you sought others to encourage them?

The next time you meet a stranger, remember, they may need a simple word of encouragement to get them through to the next day. Out of your pain, bless others.

Even a stranger in a plane.

It will cure your own hurt more than you know.

 *SEEKING THE THIN PLACES...*

1. **Have you ever felt sorry for yourself and crawled into self-pity?**

2. **When is the last time you engaged someone not like you and it was a blessing to you?**

3. **Have you been so covered up by your own circumstances that others seemed not to exist?**

Entry #10

The Chariot Race and Four White Horses

It was he who gave some to be apostles, some to be prophets,

some to be evangelists, and some to be pastors and teachers,

to prepare God's people for works of service, so that

the body of Christ may be built up.

—Ephesians 4:11-12 *NIV*

orses have always fascinated me. The extreme power and speed these animals are capable of is amazing. I recall watching the Kentucky Derby in 1973 and marveling at a horse named Secretariat. I didn't know at the time I was witnessing history. As it turns out, I was watching the most famous racehorse ever.

They called Secretariat "Big Red" because he was larger than most other racehorses (he stood 16 hands 2 inches and weighed 1,175 pounds). After he died, the autopsy revealed that his heart was literally twice the size of the other horses in the field. His owner, Penny Chenery, said that he had twice the power plant for fuel and a will to win that was driven by competition.

Secretariat won the Kentucky Derby that year by 2½ lengths and set the track record (1:59.40), which still stands today. The most amazing thing about it was that he ran each quarter-mile segment faster than the one before it. That means he was still accelerating into the final quarter-mile of the race!

The next Triple Crown event was the Preakness Stakes. Secretariat broke last, but was leading after the first turn. He won that race by 2½ lengths as well.

Ron Turcotte was Secretariat's jockey, and he understood more than anyone else what gifts this incredible horse possessed. Turcotte knew how he broke from the gate, whether he liked the rail or the outside, whether he preferred to lead early or lay back and make his move late. He knew how Big Red thought, and he knew what would make this horse a legend.

Secretariat may have won most of the races he ran in, regardless of who sat in the saddle. But understanding his strengths and weaknesses, his likes and dislikes, made Secretariat unbeatable. Turcotte knew that Secretariat loved competition, loved running against the best.

"He loved to look into the eyes of the other horse just before he hit the afterburners," Turcotte said. The only race that caused anxiety for both the jockey and Big Red's owner was the Belmont Stakes.

The Belmont is a race that requires endurance and timing more than just sheer speed. Because of its length and because it is the final race of the Triple Crown, it is called the "Test of the Champion." It tests a horse's heart and his will to win, if he can go the distance. Secretariat won that race as well, by an astounding 31 lengths, and ran the fastest 1½ miles on dirt in history…2:24.00 flat. It's a record that stands to this day.

The thing about a horse like Secretariat is that he was built to run—nothing else. He was not made to pull like a draft horse or round up cattle like a cutting horse. He was designed to do one thing and was trained to use his strengths: speed and power. He maximized what gifts he had and made them work. And still today, his name is legendary.

What about us? Are we using our strengths in this race called life? Or are we chasing after something we weren't designed for? Maybe you were built for something completely different. If you're built to pull, you're not going to be very effective on the racetrack. If you're built to run, you're going to be spinning your wheels in front of a heavy load.

You see, I think sometimes we try to do things we weren't meant to do. Work in areas where we aren't gifted. On the other hand, we all have specific gifts we've been given, yet we either don't recognize them or we don't know how to use them for our own good or the good of others. Imagine Secretariat working in a field, pulling a plow. Could he do it? Absolutely! But that's not the question. Was he designed to do it? That's the real question.

Of all the movies that have been made involving horses, *Ben-Hur* has to be my favorite. Do you know what scene I love to watch over and over again? Not the chariot race. That's what you were thinking. Nope. It's the scene when Judah Ben-Hur meets these four white Arabian horses for the first time.

Arabians are considered one of the premier horses in the world for endurance. They are strong, sleek, fast, smart, and built to do almost anything required of them. The four Arabians in the movie are stunning. They are trained to pull a chariot and one driver for the biggest race of their lives, and they receive the best of everything. After all, they belong to an Arab sheik.

Judah Ben-Hur, a/k/a Charlton Heston, sees them for the very first time. He is mesmerized by their beauty and strength. He finds them trying to walk in a circle side by side, just like they will need to do in the chariot race, except they will be running flat out. The race is long and requires 100 percent commitment from each horse. These horses will be running as hard as they can for the entire race—no jogging or taking a lap off. Run hard and run smart. With other chariots in the race, some maneuvering will be asked of these great creatures. It won't be a straight path. That means that speed and agility are physical requirements for each horse.

The sheik that owns these four creatures, oddly enough, is having a difficult time getting them to work with one another. Curiously, the horses seem to dislike one another. They seem to be biting at one another. They seem to be uncomfortable and agitated just by walking together. What would happen when they started running?

The viewer soon finds out why these horses are so uncomfortable. They're out of place. They are positioned in the wrong spot to pull this chariot. If you're like me, you're asking, "What's the difference? Just pull the chariot. Don't worry about what position you're in. How tough can it be?"

Ben-Hur had a love and appreciation for horses and recognized what was wrong by watching them maneuver in a circle. He explained to the sheik that they were out of place. Even though they all looked the same, acted the same, were the same breed, and had the same high energy, the same heart and will to win, something was different, something was wrong.

The horses knew they were out of place, out of their comfort zones, but didn't know where they belonged or how to get there. Ben-Hur notices that the horse running on the inside has the longest legs. The chariots raced on an oval track, going counter-clockwise, like a modern-day racecar. That means the horse on the outside would cover more ground than the others and would need longer legs to make the turn efficiently. Therefore, the outside horse was running on the inside, out of position.

Next, he observed the horse on the outside had a large chest and shorter legs. He would be far more effective on the inside, to anchor the weight of the chariot and to make the inside turn. This horse was also out of position.

The two horses in the middle needed guidance. In the herd, they would be followers, not leaders. During the race, they needed a horse on each side of them. What they do best is run, with no obligations to anchor or turn; they just want to pull and run.

Ben-Hur's suggestion to the sheik is a lesson we can all learn from. In fact, it's profound. It's all about the sweet spot. An "ace in its place." It's about running a race but making sure you're in position. Being in a place where you can live life to the fullest.

Have you ever experienced "being out of place"? You may have looked the part, but you weren't in the right spot? From the outside looking in, everything seems to fit. You've got the skills, you're doing a good job, and people are telling you what you want to hear. But deep-down inside, you know it's not your calling. You run anyway, but you're not satisfied. You may even claim victory, but you remain empty inside because you were just "going through the motions."

You see, God is calling you for something in this life, but until you find your place—your giftedness—you'll be running the race out of position. What if your life's work, your calling, matched your giftedness exactly? Would life seem different? Would it be more challenging? Or more exciting? Are you running on the inside but built for the outside? Are you following but deep inside you know you should be leading?

Looking back on that movie with this insight, it's obvious that each horse is gifted differently, and there's only one way they can pull successfully as a team. They've got to know their position and find their place. What's interesting is that even out of position it's conceivable that they could have won the race. But they would have been distracted, agitated, and uncomfortable while doing it. That's why keeping track of "wins" and "losses" is not God's idea of success—it's all about the sweet spot!

Have you ever wondered how some ordinary people can accomplish extraordinary things? Wondered why a smarter more capable you has not realized that kind of success? Do you compare yourself to others and get discouraged because they're "farther along" than you are? Have you settled for less than what you were designed to do?

Perhaps one of the thin places in life is when you realize—without a doubt—what kind of race you're in, what kind of life you're called to live, what kinds of gifts you were given, what you were designed for…and then, you act on it. The apostle Paul wrote that we all have unique gifts. The thing is, we need each other to use our gifts. We need leaders, followers, teachers, givers, prophets, encouragers, exhorters, healers. We need each other to use our gifts and to become what we were truly intended to be in this life.

Looking back on the chariot race scene, one of the camera shots tells the story of finding your place, of running in position. It comes during the most exciting part of the race. It's a close-up of the four horses, running at full speed in perfect unison. Pulling in rhythm and motion. Their nostrils are as large as half dollars sucking in all that air to keep pace and running like they were born to do.

For me, I found my position in this race called life just a few years ago. I was running on the inside and covering less ground than I was designed to cover. I needed to run on the outside, but I needed others with completely different gifts and strengths that I don't possess to make what I do a success.

I need constant grooming, constant encouragement. Above all else, I need someone who truly loves me for who I am, for what I bring to the race—a God that seeks to encounter me in thin places, to reveal who He has made me to be in Christ. What about you?

Find your passion. Live your dream. Embrace your calling, and go for it. It could be the greatest chariot race you ever run. I always felt I was supposed to serve in the church. So, I served in various positions, thinking that I was in the right place. But I was like those horses, distracted and, at times, uncomfortable. It took a season of wandering and deep reflection, but I discovered that God was leading me to the place I was supposed to be. When I took my eyes off the circumstances of my life and replaced worry with worship, it became clear. I was designed for something much different. Today, God has blessed me beyond measure by moving me into the right position. And it has made all the difference in the world.

Ben-Hur drove those horses to victory because he understood their capabilities, their giftedness. But only after each of them was repositioned to run and live the way they were designed to run. Ben-Hur knew those Arabians…Turcotte knew Secretariat…God knows you.

Are you ready to run?

SEEKING THE THIN PLACES...

1. **What gifts do you feel you have that you're not using presently?**

2. **In your work, in your marriage, as a parent, as a single person, as someone who desires to live out a passion, are you utilizing your gifts and passions to best help others?**

3. **If out of position, how do you get in the right position to run the race you were meant to run?**

Entry #11

Did Your Father Ever Come to Your Football Games?

Our limitations and success will be based, most often, on our own expectations for ourselves. What the mind dwells upon, the body acts upon.

—Denis Waitley

Perhaps more than any other entry, this story pierces my heart the deepest. I still struggle with it today, every day. I can't explain why it still bothers me, or perhaps I should say "haunts" me. It just does. I struggle with it at various times. It creeps in on me like a wolf in the night when my attitude is most optimistic. It pays me a visit and harnesses my spirit when things in my life are going well.

Funny thing—it reminds me that looking to the past pays little dividends.

It tugs on me to look back at circumstances that I can no longer change. Trust me, when that happens, your life stalls. Your future seems to look less and less because your past reminds you of struggle.

I read a billboard the other day outside a local church. It said:

"If you keep dwelling on the past your life will be history."

This is simple logic, isn't it? You think in the past, you will live in the past. For me I was trying to please a father that is no longer around. Trying to live up to someone's expectations is hard to do—living their dreams and ambitions for your life, not yours. How do you win that battle?

Have you experienced this in your life? It has the potential to damage you beyond what you could imagine. A battle you can't win.

Years ago, I was working on staff at a local church. I had just been through an Alpha class where the teacher made it interesting and understandable. He had also been my prayer partner for nine months.

Alpha is a class designed to spark questions about God from unbelievers. It's a ten- to fourteen-week course. I was a table leader. Every table has a leader that is knowledgeable about God. These leaders are there just to keep the questions coming in hopes of God revealing Himself over time to the participant.

After the course was over, several weeks went by. One of the pastors on staff came to me and asked if I would teach the next Alpha class. What a great opportunity!

I had never taught it before, but this would be a chance for me to help the cause of Christ.

This was about the people I would talk to over the weeks.

This was about planting a seed so God could come and water it in the future.

This was about being up to bat for God, about being up close and personal with people to watch what God could do in their lives, about truly witnessing a life-changing moment for them.

Or so it seemed. What I have found over the years is whom God has chosen for the lesson and whom I have chosen are not the same.

The week before the class started, I began to watch all the videos and read all the notes on the class. It was a crash course on teaching this curriculum the most effective way. I studied and studied. I watched the video over and over. I rehearsed in the mirror. I took seven pages of notes just to make sure I didn't forget anything that would be of great value to them.

Sunday came and I was ready!

My wife went with me. I love to have her along because she will always be truthful to me in her critique of my delivery. I'm used to it. She has a way of letting me know what was good and what was not so good. I look forward to her comments after my talks.

The Alpha course was being held in a room larger than in the past. Why? There were seventy-three people signed up for the class. It was unusual to have that many at one time. I thought nothing of it other than it was just a way for me to reach others with a creation story that would challenge them from all angles, just on a much larger scale. The class was large and the class would offer a way for many, through what I would say, to learn about God.

Day 1. Off I went. I had my notes, my Bible, my lectern. I spoke for almost an hour. It was great! I covered everything I wanted to cover and more. I exited, allowing the table leaders to take over for the remainder of the class time. My wife met me in the hallway, away from all the other ears.

"What was that?" she said.

Her face all frowned up and angry. I had never heard this response from her in twenty some years of marriage. I was shocked!

I did great.

I covered everything.

God would be proud.

I had delivered a message for Christ that would make anyone reflect on who this God might be. That was the goal for the class, wasn't it? And I didn't miss the mark.

"What are you trying to prove?" she asked. "That was terrible. Why do you teach like that? I don't understand. Teach like you're suppose to. Not like that."

I was just hoping that no one in the room with all those people heard her scold me. I was totally at a loss for words. Thinking you've accomplished something good only to be hammered for completely the opposite is devastating.

Bang! All this weight of disappointment hit me. What happened? As we drove home, all my efforts seemed for nothing. I couldn't do any better. How could I improve on that? I studied and studied. It felt as if I had prepared for an exam all week only to fail the final. What kept resonating in my head was the word she used—*prove.*

That stuck with me. That word implies self-indulgence, focus on the self, trying to be better than others, a missing piece that I was trying to add. The word *prove* communicated all those ideas to me. What I always try to get across is the complete opposite.

It's not about me,

it's about God,

it's all about others.

I felt sick. What I thought was a success was a failure. The devil ruined for me my intentions to please God. I worked hard. It was about works, not about faith. But a question posed to me the next day changed my outlook on ministry forever.

My wife pleaded with me to call the pastor who had taught the class right before me. She wanted me to ask him how he prepared for the class. Perhaps he could give me insight on what I had obviously missed. The next day I called to leave a voice mail for him. In the past, if he calls you back within a week, you're lucky. His schedule was that busy.

Sitting in my office, I picked up the phone and dialed his number.

"Hello?"

That never happened before. "Brother, I need to talk to you. Can I get on your calendar?"

"What about now? I'm on the church campus for a meeting," he said.

What I've come to understand when God wants you to learn something, meet someone, spend time alone only talking to Him, it will happen. For Jeff to pick up the phone on the first ring was a miracle. To be available right then at that moment was God.

I met him outside the church on the front lawn. We both sat on the brick wall that led to the main doors to the church entrance. It being Monday, it was just the two of us. I began to explain.

"You won't believe what happened when I taught the Alpha class yesterday. I had seven pages of notes, I saw the video at least six times, I cross-referenced all the verses in the Bible just in case they had lots of questions, I had backup notes for all the table leaders. I spoke for about an hour. There was nothing else I could have said for it to be any better."

He paused. He waited. Then he looked dead into my soul. For some crazy reason I felt a question coming that I wouldn't like. As this strange feeling began to cover me, he asked,

"Did your father ever come to your football games?"

It seemed like the next few seconds turned into hours. A lump in my throat swelled up, and I could no longer see Jeff clearly with my own eyes. Tears came rolling down my cheeks.

I said nothing. It all hit me at once.

The one question that could paralyze me,
my faith,
my calling,
my commitment to God,
my life in ministry came crashing down around me.

Reality and truth have a way of doing that. If you think about it, the question he asked had nothing to do with the Alpha class. One thing I need to let you know. Jeff had been my prayer partner in the past for about nine months. He had heard every word coming out of my heart. He heard all the joys and all the pains and concerns. He had heard through my prayers that I was still trying to please a dad that was no longer around. I hadn't actually said that, but he knew. He put two and two together. Jeff said little in those months of praying together. He picked the perfect time to make a point that I would never forget.

All the hard work, studying, preaching, teaching, presentations in meetings…

It had become my motivation in life…to please a dad that was gone. I based all my studies, all my marriage, all my relationships, all my spiritual and ministry callings on trying to prove I was worthy to be where I was.

I was looking for confirmation that I was accepted. Have you ever been there before? Are you still there? What I have come to know is that I have never received an answer of confirmation from my dad all these years. He's been gone since 1980. I never will receive it. You see the viscous cycle I was on?

Jeff had hit the mark in one sentence. He knew I always wanted my father to come to my football games, and he never did. Reason being, his work demanded much from him. He was always giving time to others, and I was somewhere down the list. He loved me, no question. But you spell love many different ways. One of those ways is *t-i-m-e*.

God spoke to me through Jeff during months of prayer time. God was patient in getting me to realize that proving my value to others is not the way to go. That I have only one true Father, and God is who that is.

What I have also come to realize is when encountering a thin place in life...

"You never see it coming."

The woman at the well never saw it coming.

Moses at the burning bush never saw it coming.

Zacchaeus in the sycamore tree never saw it coming.

Abraham sacrificing his son Isaac never saw it coming.

Peter, James, and John, on the Mount of Transfiguration, never saw it coming.

Saw what coming? A one-on-one genuine encounter with the Creator of the universe. Who plans for that?

Today I have changed one thing about how I approach life. I am fully aware that I can have the sudden motivational drive to please a dad that is no longer there. It creeps in like a lion in the night. It's quick and robs me of all the joy in Christ I could be experiencing otherwise.

The conversation on the front lawn that day has made me aware of several questions I always ask myself:

Whom am I pleasing?

Why do I do what I do?

To what end?

Whom do I want to get the credit?

I am no longer waiting for my dad to come through the gate with his ticket to watch me play. I love him more than ever and miss him each day that life continues on. But now God used another person with a message to clearly teach me that He is who I live for.

Looking back, the conversation lasted for almost an hour. He told me what I needed to do to prepare for the next class. No notes, only watch the video one time, and pray. That seemed as if I was not preparing enough. I still debated and questioned why this way. To prepare little is not saying you are not being faithful to God. Sometimes God prepares you for the task in which only He can supply the victory. He alone receives the credit. It had nothing to do with me.

Just show up! I went home and did exactly as he said. I had never felt more unprepared the next Sunday. As I walked in to speak, I had only my Bible. No notes to look at just in case things went wrong. I was on a high wire with no safety nets. What would I do if the message stalled?

My wife once again sat in the back of the room. I could see the top of her head, not her face. I only wanted to see the top of her head because her face told me everything I needed to know or didn't want to know.

I finished the talk, wiping sweat from my face. She met me in the hall just like she had the previous week. I felt as if the talk was the worst I had ever delivered. Was I ready for what she would say? If she said it was horrible again this time, it wasn't my fault. I did what Jeff had said to do.

Her face was beaming with a huge smile. "That was the best I have ever heard," she said.

I didn't understand. It was terrible.

"Could you hear yourself?"

I thought I did, but evidently I didn't.

"The words were simple, the message was clear, their choices were well defined."

It had nothing to do with me. God is simple. His message was clear. The choice we have to make today is well defined. No smoke and mirrors, no trap doors, no performance needed to earn your way. Just be faithful in the cause and God will do all the work.

I still think about my dad. His pictures are on my desk right now. In one he is a young Navy recruit back in WWII. The other is later in life, sitting at his desk, talking on the phone. I feel as if he watches me every day as I live my life getting closer and closer to where he is.

But now, I no longer look for him to punch his ticket to watch me play. God sees all my games. He is there every time I suit up for battle. "*Just show up*," God says. "*I'll be there.*" But remember, "You'll never see it coming."

SEEKING THE THIN PLACES...

1. **Is there an event in your past that haunts you to the point of "stalling" your life?**

2. **How do you overcome this and move forward?**

3. **Have you ever found yourself trying to please others at the expense of being who you really are?** If so, were you pleased at what you became?

Entry #12

"Chip, You're Preaching"

Moses said to the LORD, "O Lord, I have never been eloquent,
neither in the past nor since you have spoken to your servant.
I am slow of speech and tongue."

The LORD said to him, "Who gave man his mouth?
Who makes him deaf or mute? Who gives him sight
or makes him blind? Is it not I, the LORD?

Now go; I will help you speak and will teach you what to say."

But Moses said, "O Lord, please send someone else to do it."

—Exodus 4:10-13 *NIV*

ne of the scariest situations I have ever found myself in was to be told I was preaching and didn't know it. A packed church and a full choir have a way of intimidating the most gifted of preachers, much less someone like me. Adding to the agony was a local pastor who couldn't wait to hear what God had put on my heart to tell them as a church body. Problem was: there was not one thing to tell them.

"I didn't know I was preaching."

It was a great trip to the Philippines. I had been there many times before, but this trip was different. My wife, being from this country, made this trip all the more special. You meet friends and family you didn't know existed. Long-lost uncles I needed approval from years after I was married. Basically, they were sizing me up to see if I seemed qualified to be married to their niece. It's one thing to be married to ethnicity of your own kind, but when you marry across the lines—and for that matter across the world—the process has the ability to take sharp hairpin turns. Things I needed to eat as a rite of passage just to be considered in this family had me thinking, "Was it too late to get out of this marriage?"

The trip lasted more than two weeks. The weather was hot, and I had brought a six-member team along with me. We had ventured around the world to assist a local church south of Manila. The goal was to come alongside them and supply some leadership skills in different areas pertaining to the overall health of the church.

My wife had organized a special time at her dad's church. He had been a pastor in the Philippines. His life was influential and earned great respect around the country.

He had known the church we were partnering with.

It could hold three hundred people. The stage was large. The doors were left open all around the sanctuary because of the heat; the rotating fans seemed to never get a break.

It wasn't unusual to have roaming animals walking and flying across the sanctuary. The question to ask is what type of animal would it be? That always had me on alert.

One Sunday night, the church had come together to worship and to hear a great message. Pastor Parpa, the senior pastor, was a unique man and eloquent of speech. His children were wonderful and the church itself was vibrant in the spirit. What more could you ask?

People came from all over. Some had traveled for hours. I always wondered why people would travel so far. Were there not churches closer to where they lived? But a great speaker and man of God will draw people from all over.

The church filled to capacity; I became excited with anticipation of the coming events. The atmosphere seemed electric. The choir was in full regalia. Incredible colors. Instruments were being brought in by truck from far away so musicians could play songs that would heighten the call of worship to a fevered pitch.

I sat on the third row from the front. Our entire team sat side-by-side all the way across. As time approached the top of the hour, I took one last look around. I frankly had never seen so much enthusiasm for worship *before* worship. This was going to be great! Songs, live music, great message, and the Spirit of the Lord circling above our heads. This was the perfect atmosphere for the Lord to speak to all of us.

Several minutes before the service started, Pastor Parpa leaned over several team members and asked if I was ready.

"Ready for what?" I responded.

I thought perhaps I was picked to speak about the team and what our goal was in being there. No problem; I'll shoot from the hip.

"What do you want me to say?" I asked.

"You're preaching," he said.

I swallowed my gum sideways.

Have you ever been caught between a hard place and, well, a harder place? I saw this playing out in three ways. When you are in this kind of position, your brain thinks at warp speed.

Option one: admit I knew nothing about speaking tonight; this would make me appear unprepared, and Pastor Parpa would have to deliver the message most likely. Not good.

Option two: graciously excuse myself from speaking; this would insult not only the pastor but everyone else involved to make this night happen. Again, not good.

Option three: walk to the stage, sit beside the pastor, smile real big like I knew all along I was speaking, and then sweat in silence until it was my turn. Not good for me.

I chose option three. As I stood and walked behind the pastor to the stage, I heard the rest of the team giggling under their breath.

"What's he going to do?

"Is he crazy?"

I sat on the platform beside the pastor, and the choir began by opening with a beautiful song *a cappella*. The music was angelic. It was the type of music that only heaven could identify with.

However, it was difficult for me to enjoy because my mind was scanning for what I might say just minutes away. As I began to search my biblical memory banks, panic set in. I was in a place I had never been before, thrown into deep water without any type of life preserver.

I recall Christ telling Peter in Luke 5:4, "Put out into the deep." The word *deep* carries significant implications. Deep water is a place where comfort and routine go sailing out the window. It's difficult to navigate in deep water without instrumentation. You need something other than your own knowledge and understanding to lend a hand.

Shallow water requires only your feet touching the ground. You can walk anywhere you want, when you want. No other devices are needed to fish or live around the edges. It's about comfort, and it involves doing something you are accustomed to doing over and over. It becomes routine.

When life becomes routine, something is missing.

What about you?

Has your life become routine?

Do you wake up each day looking forward to nothing or the same old thing?

Have you become so comfortable that shallow water has become the apex of your existence?

What will it take for you to fish in deep water?

What circumstance would shake your foundations to get you to adventure out to unknown situations?

What you need to remember most is this: the sudden testing of Christ can come at any time. And, perhaps most importantly to remember,

you'll never see it coming!

Peter, James, and John fished these waters every day, perhaps for weeks at a time in the same spot. Life for them had become shallow. They knew what to expect and went about their day having never been pushed into a place that required more than they had to offer. They relied on themselves and their own ability to catch fish. Jesus said, after filling their boat to the point of tipping over, "Henceforth, you will be catching men."

This was an invitation to change their lives. To go places they had never been before. To meet people they would never encounter. To witness miracles that otherwise they would never see if they had not taken the leap into deep water. Christ was inviting them to abandon routine. To be willing in faith to push life for all it's worth. But I must warn you: there's a catch.

To venture into these deep waters is a serious risk. You risk the unknown, the unordinary, a split-second jerk of life moving in another direction. You cannot plan for what may be in front of you or, in this case, below you.

But you'll never live a more exciting life!

You see, thin places represent a layer of unexpected moments designed to change your thinking and trajectory in life. They reshuffle the deck of adventure and say, "Hang on." For me, teaching in different churches around the world is exciting and great, no doubt. But part of the preparation had become routine. All the skills it took to prep messages came mostly from the classroom in seminary. I cherish the knowledge, but no class I ever signed up for prepared me for what was before me there.

I sat waiting as if my opportunity to speak would fail me and fail God. But God visited me at the deepest of levels. He knew my fear and what it would take to get through this. How did He know? He put me there. And for the first time I couldn't rely on myself to deliver. Messages and themes sometimes take weeks to prepare, not minutes, not seconds. And as I looked out over the crowd, the stakes could not have been higher. The church was packed, and all in attendance anticipated a message from an American pastor that was dynamite. My hanky was so saturated from nerves I could have rung it out.

I sat on the platform—God made Himself known. He had me remember that this was a church my father-in-law had delivered message after message to. His spirit was all around, and I felt it more now than all the years I had lived with him in the same house. A calming hand came over me that was indescribable. My heart rate came down and fear dissipated like an early morning fog when the sun hits it. All seemed to be getting better, and then the revelation that put me firmly in the thin place God had intended all along happened.

My mother had passed away from a terrible disease months before. At the funeral, I had asked a dear friend to play on her flute my mother's favorite hymns. As I sat listening to her playing all these hymns, threading one into another seamlessly, I was taken by emotion at the wonderful life my mother had lived and the life she lived for Christ.

It just so happens that the same person who played that flute medley was one of the team members. Unknowingly to me, Pastor Parpa had asked her to be involved in the service and to play her flute. He told her to pick whatever she desired to play. Whatever it was would be a blessing to the entire church.

What do you think she chose to play?

You're right. Of all the songs she could have played, she played my mother's favorite hymn medley. As I listened in shock, I was overcome by emotion. Tears began to roll off my cheeks. I knew what was happening, and I was the recipient of this awesome gift of being used by God. Through this music, my mother's presence was felt. My father-in-law's presence was felt. I found myself surrounded by a cloud of witnesses and "family" that indirectly said to me, "We are with you. Preach, son."

God made sure that this was a moment, a thin place, where only He was in control, and whatever came out of my mouth to say to these people was not of my doing. It was God's words and His doing.

Nikki finished the three-minute medley, and all eyes turned to me. It was finally my turn. I stood and walked to the podium. The walk was some twenty feet. When I stood, I had no idea what I would speak on. Twenty feet later, when I arrived to place my Bible down, I knew exactly what God had for me to say. I can't explain it. It filled my mind at warp speed. My mind was being filled by God in the "blink of an eye." You can't measure that in seconds. I was filled by the Holy Spirit within seconds, and I preached for over an hour to all who would listen.

Looking out over the audience, I saw people grabbing for blank sheets of paper to take notes. I saw people asking for something to write with from their neighbors. And, most of all, I remember my team sitting there taking notes from what God had to say to them as fast as they could. Afterward, people came to me recalling some of my quotes and what they wrote. Frankly, I don't remember saying any of it. Don't get me wrong; the experience from beginning to end I remember quite well. But actually what I said in the heat of the message was and remains a blur in my mind.

Thin places carry with them a measure of mystery. I firmly believe that people don't share these thin places in their lives for fear they had no witnesses to confirm their stories. For me, I had over three hundred witnesses and a team member who said, "That was the best message I have ever heard." I wish I could say it was due to all the prep I had put into it. But it wasn't. God gave the message. I was just the voice that delivered it. I had been in a place so deep that only God could navigate where I was to go. In this situation, I was all-in. I had no choice.

God sometimes will put you into a place like this even when you are not willing to go on your own. Imagine what God could do with you when your attitude is, "God, whatever You desire, wherever You desire, send me."

That's when lightning strikes! It's a call to full surrender. To fish and be willing to sail into deep water. For Peter and the apostles who left their nets that day, their lives were never the same.

What about you?

Let's go fishing into deep water…

> *Pray also for me, that whenever I open my mouth,*
> *words may be given me so that I will fearlessly make known*
> *the mystery of the gospel.*

—Ephesians 6:19 *NIV*

SEEKING THE THIN PLACES…

1. **Think back to an event in your life when you were the most unprepared.** How did you react to the situation?

2. **How can you learn to fully trust God in your unprepared moments?**

Entry #13

Matthew and His Dad: Seeing the Best in Others

Every great dream begins with a dreamer. Always remember,
you have within you the strength, the patience, and the passion
to reach for the stars to change the world.

—Harriet Tubman

They say the world is about choices. Whatever comes out in the end, good, bad, or indifferent, life is simply about choices. For some, choices are generated by the inner passion of the human spirit and a desire to see the best in others. Some choose to see others in a negative light. No matter how you slice it, we have the ability to see in others what we desire to see.

When it comes to parents and their children, we should choose to be the first and last to encourage our kids in whatever they do. Sadly, parents choose on occasions to be a hindrance and a stumbling block that leave mental scars for years to come.

Some of these choices are dominated by inhibitions of the past that somehow have become a part of our decision process. The way we were raised by parents has the ability to carry over and infiltrate our actions in the most negative of ways.

But we are all born with a purpose in life. To dream and discover through this journey we call life to "become." To become what God has challenged and placed within us to become. External challenges may be different from others, but the internal struggles are very much the same. We long to be loved. We long to be loved by our own family.

The story of Matthew is a story of a dad discovering his son's desire to simply be loved and accepted. Matthew, all along, had the desire to be "unnoticed." In a world where most kids strive to be noticed, Matthew just wanted to fit in like all other kids his age and be seen as normal.

It all began on a local high school football field. I was the leader of a flag football league that was to last over several months. Each Saturday morning, coaches would arrive early as the sun was breaking over the trees. They would line the field and set up the cones to show where the end zone began and ended. The kids ranged in ages from ten to fifteen, boys and girls. They arrived in torn-up jeans and sweatshirts with logos of their favorite NFL teams.

On the first Saturday, the weather was fantastic. It was in the forties, not a cloud in the sky. The trees were showing off their early colors, and the dew shimmered on the grass in every direction.

Matthew was one of the first to arrive. He was twelve years old and had dark curly hair and eyes that looked like huge marbles that revolved on a swivel. Matthew was clearly excited to be there. His enthusiasm was bubbling out of his skin, olive-colored skin that sunbathers would give their right arms for. Observing him made you feel as if it was NFL draft day, and Matthew was hoping to be the number one choice.

His personality was as gentle as a lamb, and he made friends with the new kids as fast as they pulled into the gravel parking lot. Matthew's dad, on the other hand, was quite reserved, apparently not completely comfortable with the whole situation. I speculated that this could be a cultural thing. After all, Matthew looked as if he was from Mediterranean descent. But then I soon discovered there was more to it than that. As the other boys and girls continued to arrive, it became obvious that Matthew was physically different from all the rest. At twelve years old, he was much smaller than others his same age. He also ran and walked with a distinct limp. But that didn't seem to diminish his eagerness to participate.

I eventually learned that Matthew had been born with bone dysplasia called *diastrophic dwarfism.* This disorder has the characteristics of short limbs and other unseen orthopedic disorders. Even though Matthew seemed fine with his condition, his father was visibly struggling. His dad seemed to be searching for a niche that Matthew could enjoy; sports seemed to be the choice. However, he looked as if he were having second thoughts.

As the morning progressed, captains were chosen and teams were formed. Matthew was eventually chosen and put on a team, surprisingly to his father's dismay. I can say that because all fathers were around their children when it came to picking teams. Matthew's dad was off to the side as if purposely wanting to be disconnected.

Looking back, it felt as if Matthew's dad felt concerned that Matthew would be a hindrance to his teammates. If so, how wrong he was!

The first thing we need to keep in mind is this: there is a drastic difference between unusual and unique.

The term *unusual,* by default, seems to place limitations on people by nature. Contrary to that, the word *unique* has a positive overtone to it. To be unique is to be alone in your gifts, something you possess that others find difficult. Matthew was unique in every way. All the other children embraced Matthew from minute one. They never saw Matthew as anything less than they were.

This is why Jesus said in the book of Mark, "Let the children come to me, do not hinder them; for to such belongs the kingdom of God. Truly, I say to you, whoever does not receive the kingdom of God like a child shall not enter it" (Mark 10:14).

Children are simple, affectionate, forgiving, and teachable. They come into relationships with no presuppositions. They could teach many adults to look past all the deficiencies and to accept strictly on the basis of love.

Kids are perceptive. You think they don't know, when actually they're often way ahead of us. Body language speaks volumes to them. As parents, if you doubt their ability and their will to succeed, they know. Has that happened to you? When a parent struggled to believe in you, what was your inner self saying? Did it motivate you, or did you want to quit?

As parents, we all should strive to see our children in a transparent way: to understand and share their accomplishments as well as their failures. It's all a part of the creative process in parenting. My father once told me, "You learn much more in your failures than success will ever teach you." He was right.

On the football field that Saturday, Matthew's dad seemed to view Matthew as a son who needed to battle constantly to be accepted. His father would instruct him and, seconds later, turn to the coaches and say, "Maybe I should take him home and just let him play in the backyard by himself."

Did he want to protect his son from others and their comments, or was it something else?

For the coaches, watching this was painful. Outward expressions and words have a way of infecting and rubbing off on others. The mood on the field was strangely apprehensive. The truth is God was working through the sport of flag football to reveal that Matthew was special. Matthew had the ability to inspire others. Matthew had a way of letting others realize in a subtle way that his physical uniqueness would not hamper him from being a kid enjoying life.

When a son or daughter looks at their parents and sees in their eyes a lack of confidence in them, their own confidence level takes a direct hit. Potential and achievement in life take on a whole other meaning. Disbelief and doubt creep in, and, if you are in Matthew's shoes, this could be devastating for years to come.

Interestingly, the children never saw the situation that way. From the beginning, Matthew was always accepted and understood by the other kids, and he was having a blast. Even though Matthew wasn't a fast runner, nor big enough to be a good blocker, his teammates soon took on a goal. The goal was to have Matthew score a touchdown. In fact, it became the ultimate goal of the team, beyond even winning their games.

What we need to remember is when God chooses to use people, someone is going to receive a blessing that is immeasurable. The goal in life is to take the blessings we've been given and use them to bless others, right? Contrary to this, keeping what God has blessed us with and not blessing others usually leads to a dead-end road. That's why I firmly believe many wealthy people are miserable in life. They have all they want and remain empty. The line "It's better to give than to receive" has truth written all over it.

Amazingly, Matthew was blessing others and changing the way a father views him without him even knowing. God works that way too. You may not know at the time you are blessing others. But, in reality, you may have changed the life trajectory of onlookers without you knowing it.

Finally, the day came that God had planned for all along. All the kids, the coaches, and moms and dads were attending the final day of the season. God could not have scripted the day any better. Matthew's team was playing to end the season. The audience was all around the field. Matthew had yet to score all year. But you know what, he didn't care. He was being all he could be with what God had blessed him with. He was satisfied with what he had and was making a difference in the lives of others.

I think the question to be asked of all of us is, with what we have, what are we doing with it?

Are we sitting on our treasure, or are we giving it away to others?

Do we feel that we need "much" to bless others?

How much do we need to possess to bless others?

I have always laughed at couples when they say, "When we have enough money, we'll start a family." Come on! What's that figure, and how did you reach that sum total? Imagine if you took what you had, no matter how small, and began to make a difference in the lives of others.

The hard fact is Matthew has done more to impact the lives of others, young and old, than some of us in our middle ages. You see, I would always like to have the attitude of Matthew. No matter what I have, I can bless others.

Is what we have contagious?

Do we want others to grasp what we have?

Do we strive to always keep others first?

For some people, the last thing they want is for others to observe them and do what they do. The apostle Paul said something that I would never have the guts to say. He said, "Imitate me" (1 Cor. 4:16 NIV).

The weight of that request requires serious inspection into one's character and integrity. He is saying:

Treat others like I do, love others like I do, forgive others like I do, bless others like I do. That's serious. How many of us would say, "Imitate me"?

As the game was winding down, the moment came. It was what we had all waited for without saying. As the ball floated toward Matthew's hands in the corner of the end zone, his dad's face filled with emotion. Somebody had blown the coverage downfield, and Matthew was all by himself. The football hit his hands; Matthew grasped the ball as if life itself depended on it. He crossed the goal line and won the game for his team.

What a moment! Matthew was happy and laughing just like kids normally do. But in that instant, I saw that it wasn't so much Matthew who needed to believe in himself as it was his dad who desperately needed to believe in his son.

Of course when Matthew caught the ball, all the players congratulated him for scoring. But in this moment, a thin place emerged where God met a father in an unordinary way playing an ordinary game. Perhaps for the first time, his dad came to the realization that Matthew was like all other kids—the same and accepted, yet unique in his own way.

We must remember that all of us have dreams—dreams of being and becoming something more than we are. Erwin McManus said, "Impossible dreams can set in motion a chain of events resulting in a seemingly insignificant person living an extraordinary life. We are capable of more than we think."[1]

Dreams fuel the very passion that we seek. Passion is measured by the size of one's heart, not by one's physical size. As parents we need to remember that in God's eyes children are looked upon as a special gift from Him. If physical abilities were measured by God, David would never been chosen by God to take on the giant.

Imagine, a simple shepherd boy living a mundane and ordinary life finds himself a king chosen by God. Oftentimes the unexpected becomes the fingerprint of God.

Whatever happened to Matthew and his dad? I am not certain. But I can say that a parent found and embraced a son that day who had the heart of a lion. And that dad began to dream dreams of greatness for his very unique son.

Parents need to be their children's greatest supporters. Parents are to be the ones who believe in their children when no one else does. Attend every game or rehearsal, no matter what the circumstance. When the world ignites despair and doubt in the eyes and hearts of children, parents are the voice of hope and the greatest reason why God made us.

---

1   Erwin Raphael McManus, *Soul Cravings* (Nashville: Thomas Nelson, 2008), 88.

SEEKING THE THIN PLACES...

1. **You're unique to God.** Do you see yourself and your gifts the same way?

2. **Kids wanted to be around Matthew.** Do others desire to be around you?

3. **Is your attitude toward life contagious to others?**

Sandy: A Boy After God's Own Heart

When angels visit us, we do not hear the rustle of wings,
nor feel the feathery touch of the breast of a dove;
but we know their presence by the love they create in our hearts.

—Anonymous

I'm in my late forties.

If Sandy were alive today, he would be my age.

I know because he was a classmate of mine in high school and a great friend. Sandy has been gone from our presence physically for some thirty years. But his memory and life remain in the minds and lives of many.

Many of us could possibly make this claim about people we knew in the past. People who continue to touch and influence our lives in a positive way long after they have departed. That's a gift from God. Sandy was, and continues to be, a gift to many.

For me, the day Sandy stepped in front of the microphone feels like it happened yesterday. Sandy's locker was near mine. His smile would light up a hallway in a split second. His classmates loved to be around him. He rubbed off on people. He had sandy blond hair, piercing eyes, a track runner's body—sleek and thin with long limbs, a picture of health. He had the heart of a lion, but, eventually, that same heart would cost him his life.

We all have friends in high school. Some people refer to groups of friends as "cliques." The same old friends, no matter where we are. In school or out on the town, Friday night football games or, in the '70s, disco nights in the cafeteria, our same group of guys or gals were always within earshot. In Sandy's case, he had friends, lots of them. Everyone in the school was his friend. Not because he tried to make everybody his friend but because they were drawn to him. He had a voice and personality you could approach. Students hovered around him like a celebrity.

He was outgoing, good looking, and accepting of others no matter who they were; he treated everyone the same; he was an encourager; he sympathized and empathized with whatever trials his classmates brought to him. He gave them his personal time to a fault. He was a great listener. He was a model student. His laugh was contagious, and he loved people.

He loved all people.

Building relationships with people for a lifetime was his true gift. He never shunned anyone. He saw in people what others failed to see or recognize. He constantly saw potential in everyone he encountered. Sound familiar? He went out of his way to help others. He considered himself less than everyone else. And he had all that at the early age of seventeen.

He will forever be young.

Sandy was the son of Dr. Leighton Ford, who is the brother-in-law of Dr. Billy Graham. Sandy carried with him a huge responsibility because of his heritage.

Although I know it would have made no difference to him one way or the other. He was just who he was, period.

I recall a new student on his first day. A student designated to show incoming students around brought him over to meet Sandy. There was a group of us standing in front of the lockers, and Sandy was grabbing his books for the day. "Hey, Sandy, I want you to meet a new student." Sandy's face lit up with this huge smile as he gave the new student this incredible welcome, as if this guy were the only student in the school.

When you encountered Sandy, to him you were all that mattered. His attention was with no one else. You had his full attention. As the bell rang, students scampered off to class. Sandy asked the student what his lunch schedule was and suggested perhaps they could grab lunch together. This kid was amazed. As Sandy left to go to class, this guy looked as if whatever premonitions and fears he had when he arrived left just as quickly as they came. Sandy made him at home.

He was that way with all the students. I remember his dad asking me years later to tell him stories about Sandy that perhaps he had never heard. I told him of this story.

He became emotional as I expect any dad would upon hearing how his son encouraged others. I told him anyone who met Sandy was a better person after they had encountered him. His voice was soothing and his thoughts were deep. But, no matter what, he never talked over your head. He spoke to you where you were in life. He cared about your personal stories. He always said everyone has a story to tell, and he loved to hear each one.

In our senior year Sandy was running to be the president of the student counsel. Sandy was in the mix with some eight other students. All were qualified for the spot and popular with all the students. The day came when the entire student body would assemble in the gym to hear the candidates' campaign speeches. Each would be allowed three minutes to make a case for why they should get the students' votes. In those days every student could fit in the gym.

The bell rang alerting all the students to report to the gym. All the teachers were present, the principal and assistant principal were there, all the counselors and coaches were sitting with the faculty. What a stage on which to make a campaign speech. I remember where I was sitting. I could go there now and sit in the exact same spot. Three rows of bleachers off the floor and right at the twenty-five yard line is where you would have found me.

Looking to my direct left, underneath one of the basketball baskets, a podium was wired with a microphone. Eight of my peers had speeches in hand. Stanley Mackey was the first to speak. Debra Thompson was next. They both gave their three-minute pitches and sat down. Next was Jim Henderson, who eventually studied at Duke University. Then came one other—the name escapes me. I am in my late forties, you know. I can't remember everything.

Sandy spoke last. Anybody that was anybody was present. The entire student body, as well as the guys who swept the floors of our school were there. The stage was set to hear a great speech from Sandy. Sandy stood and walked behind the mic. He had three sheets of paper in hand to let us know his speech for student body president was well thought-out.

As he began, he took all three sheets he supposedly had his speech on and tossed all of them to the floor. They landed like trash. The gym fell dead silent. He stood and looked over everybody from one end of the gym to the other, silently. His silence seemed like hours. *What is he doing? Is he crazy? Is he scared? Maybe he changed his mind?* These were the comments of students sitting near me. I wondered myself. Finally, Sandy began.

"Thank you for being here today. I don't care anything about being president of the student body of this school. I respect the other candidates who share this platform with me; they are my friends. Whomever you elect, they will all make a great class president. But for me, all I care about is where you will spend your life for all eternity. That is the most important thing for me, and I have you for the next three minutes."

I gasped as did all the other students in the gym. Teachers' mouths were swung open as if they were sitting in the dentist chair. Coaches looked at one another. The principal, Mr. Rosell, was perplexed as to what to do. Should he stop Sandy or let him go? Sandy planned well his time to speak. Not only did he use the time to speak for Jesus, but also he knew everybody would be there and he would have an audience like never before. He used all three minutes to share the gospel of Jesus and what they needed to do to have the same salvation he had.

He ended his message by saying, "Eternity is at stake."

Students were moved beyond themselves. Sandy had touched a nerve that pinged like sonar deep in their souls. This guy was not kidding. He really cared. He hit us full throttle and deep, challenging us to ask the hard question concerning our lives. Some student faces looked as if they were talking to themselves, asking the question already. If Sandy thought this was a serious question, perhaps everyone should give it some serious thought too.

I have always said that when God comes to you in a thin place, "you never see it coming."

It's quick.

It will test you.

It will ask you the hard questions.

It has the ability to change your life.

Sandy's message was all the above. God shows up in many ways, and this had all the ingredients of one of those very thin places.

Sandy asked these questions with a certain focus in mind. Sandy was focused on them, his friends, not himself. Sandy was focused on the eternal, not the here and now. He saw the big picture with eternal implications, not the immediate gratification for himself and others. Mark Batterson, in *Primal,* asks the question we all need to ask ourselves: "Are you focused on your wants or others' needs?"[1]

That's really the question, isn't it?

Sandy thrived on it.

We should as well.

He finished his speech, and then walked back to his chair with a standing ovation from all. I have never witnessed a person who was so willing to put their faith on the line for God. Today, thirty years later, students still talk about it. Some had their lives changed by it. That's eternal investment.

What about you?

Right now, are you investing in someone with your time?

Are you encouraging someone who desperately needs to hear an encouraging word from you?

Your focus is tied directly to where your heart is. Where your heart is determines your passion. Your passion gives birth to compassion and joy that burst through like a fountain of spiritual contentment. What you've realized like Sandy is that time is short. Life, even if you live to be of old age, passes quickly. How many times have you heard aging people say, "The older I get, the faster time goes by."

---

1   Mark Batterson, *Primal: A Quest for the Lost Soul of Christianity* (Colorado Springs: Multnomah Books, 2009), 37.

Interesting, isn't it? They sense time moving faster and faster, but is it really? Nope. Older people feel time is short, that their chances of being around decrease year after year.

For Sandy, his time was shorter than anybody knew. Sandy, as I mentioned before, ran track. He was good. He pushed himself to the limits every time he ran. I still look at pictures of him in my annual running on the track. The picture of him falling on the track still sends chills through me. You see, Sandy had a heart condition. He knew it was there. He knew, and he still pushed himself to live life for all it was worth.

Graduation took place in the summer of 1979. Sandy went off to college, and I moved away. I stayed in touch with him somewhat but, looking back, not often enough. I received a phone call one day telling me that Sandy was going into surgery at Duke for his condition and to pray for him. Sandy was a warrior, so I knew God had him in the palm of His hand. Not to worry. Sandy would be fine and live a great life for Christ.

The next day I received a call from one of my high school classmates.

Sandy had passed away. I was stunned and saddened beyond explaining. But I was told that before he went into surgery he had left a letter on his bed for his family to read. It's as if he knew he would not be coming back.

Today, many years later, Sandy continues to affect and "infect" my life. His life was contagious, and I try to catch what he had. He was bold beyond measure. He put his trust in God. Whatever God wanted to do with his life was OK with Sandy. He lived life every day like it was his last.

What about you?

Most likely you don't have the condition Sandy had. But...

Are you acting as if time were short?

Imagine if we did.

Would it change our way of living and our priorities?

Are you being contagious to the point where others desire what you have?

Sandy changed the way students think for the rest of their lives. I know; I've talked to them. They decided on that day to make a decision to follow Christ. So many lives have never been the same.

What about you? Have you decided where you will spend eternity? You will spend it somewhere, why not with the Creator of all things who loves you to the point of giving His life for you?

For just three years, God gave me the friendship of Sandy Ford. This friendship taught me not to waste time. You never know when today may be your last. How I encounter God in these thin places has eternal consequences. Sandy was there and then he was gone. Some friendships and encounters that seem like a flash, and then they disappear. Yet they leave us knowing we have been with God if for only a brief period of time—a thin place.

If this story about Sandy has touched you to the point of making a decision for Christ, don't read another word until you settle where your eternity will be lived.

It's that important!

I will see Sandy again one day. I am looking forward to that reunion. I have much to tell him, and I will have all eternity to do that.

SEEKING THE THIN PLACES...

1. **Sandy had three minutes to talk.** If you had three minutes in front of a captive audience, what would you tell them of your faith?

2. **Do you consider yourself an encourager?** If not, what gift best describes you and how might that help others?

3. **Life is short.** Do you live it knowing that fact? What would you need to change to adopt this attitude?

A Voice from the Back Row

And if he finds it, truly, I say to you, he rejoices over it
more than over the ninety-nine that never went astray.
So it is not the will of my Father who is in heaven
that one of these little ones should perish.

—Matthew 18:13-14

Years ago, I was teaching a Sunday school class in a local church outside of Philadelphia. It was a way for me to stay close to God and hone my skills of research. Most of all, it allowed me to invest in others. I studied each week, preparing messages to further the group's biblical knowledge. Though it was exciting, something was missing in my spirit. For some deep and unnerving reason, my spirit felt empty. Don't get me wrong. As I said, the time spent studying benefited me perhaps more than it helped the ones receiving my words. Still, one of my spiritual cylinders was not firing.

One day, a lady whom I knew from a distance came to the class. Mrs. Bealor was middle-aged and seen as a catalyst member of the church. After the class one

Sunday, she waited to speak to me off to the side. "It's so nice to meet you," she said. "I enjoyed the class."

"I am glad you liked it. Please feel free to come again."

She never did.

But my relationship with her for the next several years changed me for the rest of my life. She attended my class one time. Just one time. Then never again. It turned out to be a visit from a very thin place. I never saw it coming.

Have you ever had encounters with people that changed you for the rest of your life?

One simple conversation that sent you off into another direction?

Did it make you refocus where you were and what you were doing in the whole scheme of things?

One person,

one conversation,

one encounter?

Simply, God heard my cries and He acted. Thin places are about God acting and reacting on your behalf. God Himself breaks into human history in various ways. It doesn't have to be God Himself. God comes in all kinds of forms. Just read the biblical stories: a pillar of fire at night, a cloud in the day, and angels sent your way to give you a word directly from the throne, all with the aim of impacting your life in a positive way.

As all the others disappeared after the class, Mrs. Bealor and I continued to chat. She asked if I liked speaking in front of people. Did I feel comfortable? She said my voice carried across a room without losing much volume. I suppose that was a compliment; at the time I wasn't sure. I had no idea what she was getting at or what she did for a living. I had only met her an hour before.

"What are you doing this afternoon around four o'clock?" she said.

"Ah…not sure. What do you have in mind?" I answered.

She began to explain to me that she had been directing live stage plays for years. She was asking if I would come and read for a "small" part in a show. Are you kidding? I've never been on stage in my life, and memorizing lines is not one of my gifts.

But I showed up. I drove to the reading thinking, *This is so ridiculous. It doesn't make sense.* God never makes sense when He's about to act and request something of us outside our comfort zones.

I read for the part among a group of other actors around a table. Mrs. Bealor asked if I would read another part on page eighty-two. I read and then I read for another part on a different page. The entire reading lasted about two hours.

As the reading session came to an end, she said, "I'll call you in a week and let you know what I have decided." Honestly, I didn't give it a second thought.

The experience was fun, but the truth is, we can't see the future like God does. There are lots of reasons for this, and let me give you one by asking a question: If we knew ahead of time what God was asking of us, would we do it? You're probably saying, "Depends on what it is."

Guess what? If God is asking something from you, you can bet it's a request that's far and above your comfort zone.

Fear would cancel out some of us. Lack of confidence would cancel out some of us. Feeling unworthy to carry out what was being asked of us would cancel out some of us. Disbelief in God's ability to set us up for success would cancel out most of us. That's the reality, is it not? We get caught in the routines of life and bicker about it until the cows come home, but when we desire something to happen in our lives and God acts, we hesitate to the point of apathy.

Apathy? That's neutral. You don't go backward, but you don't go forward either. You just sit there blaming others for your dull existence. God calls us to much more than that. Is your attitude sitting on go? Are you ready to shift into overdrive when God comes calling?

Well, the call came a week later, and I answered the phone. She began by saying that it was great to have me read. I already had in my mind that it was fun, but that's all it was, a time where I could read for a part and that's the end of that. Hey, I stepped out in faith, right? I was satisfied. My comfort level was not compromised too badly. I was content to fish around the edges in shallow water.

Are you fishing in shallow waters?

Is your comfort level so good that to rock it would make you motion sick?

If this is the case, God needs to throw you in the deep end. For me, the deep end was seconds away. "I would like for you to play the lead role in the show," she said.

"I'm sorry? What did you say? The lead?"

One of the great characteristics of God is that when you think you have the courage to answer the bell, He takes it to another level. Let's fish in the deep. I was scared to death. Teaching in front of people is not a stretch; it can become shallow water. Memorizing lines and performing is a completely different gift. Perhaps you're living a life that only scratches the surface of what you truly can do.

What would happen if you lost your life only to gain it? To turn lose of the wheel and let God drive you where you need to go?

Reluctantly, I said yes. I had the script in hand, and when I hung up the phone I started highlighting my lines on each page. They were everywhere—838 of them.

"Serious?" my wife said. "What are you doing? You've never done this before. The entire show is riding on your back."

Thanks for the confidence. The next stop for me was the bathroom. When my nerves get bad, that's where I go.

The memorizing was tough, I have to admit. I had to look at lines every day for hours. I've heard that once you have the lines down, that's when the real fun in acting begins. That's right. I started to think, *Anything God calls us to takes preparation.* If I was to be faithful in the small things, God will trust me in the much bigger things. The question was this: What were the bigger things?

Several months later, I preformed the show a number of times. I felt as if I had been missing something in my life. I should have been doing this all along. I loved it. The costumes, the stage decorations, the robe changes, the music, the playbills with my name in them. How cool is that? It was all in preparation for something down the road. I couldn't see it; I had no idea that's where this was going. If I had, I would have told God I don't have the skills—translate that word *skills* into *guts*—to pull it off.

Do you get canceled out of things in life without even trying? You just figure it's not in your skill set? Opportunities go zipping by, and you keep standing there wondering when life will shine on you? It's like standing on a train platform and the trains keep going by and you're not on any of them?

Fast forward ten years. I have been performing in the theater for years, and my playbills were stacking up into this huge résumé. It was fun, and I had become accustomed to the stage. But circumstances had me move from Philadelphia back home to take care of an ailing mother. I began to attend the church where I grew up. It was great reconnecting with old friends.

As I was attending a Wednesday night dinner, the director of the music program and choir approached me. He asked if I might be interested in the church's annual Christmas show. I was not familiar with it, so he told me to look at the part and give him an answer that night. Yep! That night. Remember…

when God acts in your life, you'll never see it coming.

I had no idea what was getting ready to happen. From what I could tell, it was a much larger production than I was accustomed to performing in. The part I was reading for was the lead. Here we go again. I wondered how Mr. Ledoux had found out about my acting in the past. I never found that answer. Anyway, I told him that evening that I would do it. I had not been on the stage for several years because of taking care of my mother.

The first rehearsal was the next week. When I showed up, I was in awe. The stage went from one end of the sanctuary to the other. It was the largest stage I had ever seen. It was deep. It went all the way back to the 120-member choir that was a part of the show. The show had more than 100 supporting people behind the scenes who constantly moved massive props that had been shipped in from Chicago. The stage was custom built in the front to reach out into the audience.

On the left side of the stage, there was a gap with lots of chairs. I found out that this was for the live symphony, almost a hundred-piece orchestra that would play for the show. I looked around and began to discover TV cameras throughout, manned by professionals. In the balcony was a separate sound booth that monitored our cordless mikes that fed into the well-placed speakers all around this massive stage. We were to do four shows, playing to an audience of some *three thousand* each show. It would be aired on TV throughout the week… and I had the lead.

The only way for me to have prepared for something like this was to be faithful in the small things. The theater in Philadelphia was great, but not on the scale of this. The largest audience might have been five hundred, not three thousand per show. The size of the stage might have been thirty feet wide, not all the way across a room that sits three thousand. I had never performed with an orchestra, and I had never been on TV. I was in the deep end in a big way.

Rehearsals went on for three weeks; the experience was great. People came from all over the city and beyond to see this Christmas special that had gained an incredible reputation over the years. I performed as best I could and loved every minute of it. The standing ovations at the end of each show had a way of convincing me they were coming to see me. It was easy to fall into the trap.

Losing perspective of what God has called you to do can happen fast. Our culture advocates this kind of thinking and behavior. Slogans like "It's all about you." "Step on whomever you need to in order to get to the top." "Never look back; the world is waiting." "Just do it." These lines are designed to promote self, and that's so easy to fall into.

By the time I retired from the stage I had performed in front of fifty thousand people. Seriously, I was teaching in a Sunday school class in the basement of a church outside Philadelphia. Who would have imagined God visiting me through a person I had never met to do something I had never done? Why? What was the purpose of this entire road of acting, and what did it teach me? Why would God send me down this path?

I had no idea until the last show I performed.

Knowing it was the last time I would "do" stage, the house was packed. The orchestra was great. The props and all the costumes were magnificent. It was a happening. The faces seemed unending. For the most part, many of the people were Christ followers. The show celebrated Christ and the saving grace He offers. It focused on a character coming to the understanding that Jesus was the only way. My lines to close out the show happened to be a prayer asking Jesus into my heart. I had rehearsed it over and over to the point where it became routine. For the audience, it was their first time hearing it performed. For some, it was perhaps their first time hearing that truth presented and prayed.

You see, what is concerning to God is when our lives and beliefs become routine. Prayer,

church,

the sacraments,

singing hymns.

You never know when God will hit you with something that requires you to act as if it were the first time. People are watching. They are searching for something other than what life has given them. They've been let down by the world and now seek something different, greater, more meaningful, more spiritual.

Something real.

As the show ended, I was standing backstage. I was chatting with all the other actors and exchanging words of gratitude for a job well done. From the corner of my eye, I saw one of the pastors rushing to talk with me. His words changed me for the rest of my life.

"Chip, I want you to know that the prayer you gave at the end of the show was incredible. Up in the balcony there was a guy on the back row watching. He had been riding with a motorcycle gang for years. He said he's hurt and abused people for most of his life. He decided to come tonight because of a tug in his heart."

I asked, "How do you know that?"

He answered, "He told me. He's in the back room with others, giving his life to Christ as we speak."

His was a voice from the back row. He sat in the balcony on the back row. No one would have noticed him there. But God did. A soul. A lost soul. A heart that became broken for God.

I always think of this man. I have never met him, only heard of his incredible transformation sitting on the back row in the dark. I remember when Jesus said to leave the ninety-nine behind to go and get the one. One is important to Christ.

Acting became an avenue to refine speaking skills. Memorizing and training my mind to have a photographic memory have been skills I have always used.

Imagine if Mrs. Bealor had not been in my class that day.

For one minute, imagine if I had said no to acting, to what she was offering. What God was offering. A chance to make a difference in someone's life for all eternity. This brief encounter in the basement of a church on a cold, cloudy afternoon became an avenue to reach a lost soul sitting on the back row.

Has God offered you a something in the past that you let pass by like another train? Have you encountered a thin place that changed you for the rest of your life?

Never put off what seems to be just another encounter asking you to do or be something you never imagined. God might be setting you up for something special.

You'll never see it coming.

 *SEEKING THE THIN PLACES...*

1. **Have you ever been asked to do something, and you knew it was deep water?** Did you go through with it?

2. **What opportunity in your life did you pass up and wish you hadn't?**

3. **What holds you back from being all that you can be?** Fear and lack of confidence paralyze the most gifted individual. What situation has paralyzed you in life that you can't overcome? What needs to happen to eliminate this problem?

Entry #16

"Where the Bluebirds Fly"

To laugh often and much; to win the respect
of intelligent people and the affection of children...
to leave the world a better place...
to know even one life has breathed easier
because you have lived. This is to have succeeded.

—Ralph Waldo Emerson

I've talked about good Samaritans. I've heard about good Samaritans. But I had never really discovered one. Over the past several years, I met one up close and personal, and he happened to be my neighbor.

He was vibrant. He loved life for all he could squeeze out of it. He spent time talking to others even when the subject being discussed didn't interest him. He was there for you, no matter what.

I came to know Ralph by hearing others talk about him. Family called him "Ralphie." He lived several blocks from me. Neighbors mentioned his name constantly, but I had never met him. He seemed elusive. I was asking, "Is he really a person, or is someone making all this up?" So I decided to see for myself.

One day, my wife and I were coming home from work. We always passed by Ralph's street. This time I decided to stop and knock on his door. Cold turkey, to my wife's questioning. "Should we stop without calling?" she asked.

"Why not."

I pulled in the driveway and walked to the door. It was a beautiful home underneath huge oak trees. I could hear music as I got out of the car. I knocked on the door and a voice rang out, "Come in!" I popped my head in the door. No Ralph. I still didn't know what he looked like.

"Hello! Where are you?" I shouted.

"Back here," he said.

As I made my way to the back of the house, he stood behind the counter and said, "Hey! I'm Ralph."

"Hi, I'm Chip." Awkward moment. What next? There he was, and I had nothing else prepared to say other than "I just wanted to know if you were a real person."

Our friendship never looked back.

Ralph was different from the start. He had no idea who I was, and he didn't care. He welcomed strangers right into his home and never flinched. That was the beginning of our relationship. Ralph loved the simple life, and he loved people. What a combination: life and people.

What else is there?

We passed each other in the neighborhood. Sometimes he would be walking his dog Millie. Or he would be riding in his truck with Millie sitting in the front seat, content to go anywhere Ralph was going.

My life was about to change in all kinds of directions. I needed to move some twenty miles away. I called Ralph, who knew much about houses and real estate. I asked him if he would be willing to go with me to see a house I was considering. When I called him, he was out of town visiting his family several hours up the road.

"I'll be back in town next week. Can we go then?"

"Of course," I said.

Just like he promised, he went with me. I valued his opinion, and I valued what he thought about all the surroundings of this development. He walked all through this house like he was the one buying it. He kicked every tire in the place.

In fact, I lost him after about twenty minutes. The Realtor couldn't find him. We yelled. No answer. All of a sudden, we heard a noise coming from underneath the house. He crawled out of the space, dirt all over him. "Looks pretty good under there," he spouted, as dirt flew from his mouth. I sat there looking at him, stunned. He took this serious. He was there for me. I was shaking my head as he dusted off the dirt.

Ralph was for everyone else, not himself. But he took everything in life with a grain of salt. No worries, at least it appeared that way. As time went by, Ralph and I became pretty close. We exchanged phone calls and conversations on the street. I invited him over to the house where I grew up. He stayed and chatted for a while.

He asked great questions.

He was always curious about others and their lives.

He liked to hear the stories of other people.

He marinated in those who shared their lives and hardships. And their victories.

Even in those stories of pain, he offered a listening ear and empathy.

He found value and appreciation of those who had struggled in life but persevered through it all, almost as if he were going through the same thing.

When our house didn't sell amidst the economic housing collapse, I invited Ralph over for a look. I wanted to know if he would buy my house as an investment property for him. He came over and walked all through the house. He loved it and asked what I was selling it for. I told him. As his face looked interested, I found the deep true meaning and calling of Ralph.

"Don't sell it. This house is worth more. This is retirement for you and your wife. I could buy it, but why should I make money when you couldn't?" I still recall those words as he stood in my kitchen. He said he could make money on this house, but why should he and not me? In ministry I had never met a person like him. Just giving.

He spent the next hour telling me why I should keep it. How it would benefit me down the road. That this house will come back in price, and to sell it would cause deep regret for me. "Keep it," he said. "Trust me."

Today, I still live in this house. He was so right.

I learned what Ralph did for other people in need too. He would drop everything and fix your toilet in the middle of the night. No money, just there to help. He loved it. It was in his bones. One of his tenants lost a job and could not afford to pay rent. Ralph not only gave them free rent over a period of time, but he also helped them move into the property knowing no money was being collected. He gave of himself, nothing expected in return. He loved in his own way. He gave love with no expectations.

One day, I stopped by to see him in the backyard of his home. It was a beautiful Sunday morning. The sun was bright and the leaves were moving with the wind. Ralph had bluebird boxes in his backyard. He loved nature. He studied the small things in life that really mattered. If he could look out his window and enjoy the bluebirds, that was enough. He spoke of how he tried and tried to get them to nest in his yard, but for some reason they flew to the neighbor's yard and nested there. It frustrated him to the point of trying all kinds of ideas to get them to nest in his boxes. They never seemed to take the bait.

I'm not sure what these bluebirds were waiting on. Why did they not come over to Ralph's house? As time went by, he had all kinds of questions for me about the church and missions.

"So tell me about the next mission trip," he asked.

I told him CLIMB was getting ready to launch a community center in Haiti.

His posture changed. He seemed interested. "When are you going?"

"Sometime this spring to take measurements and plan for future construction," I replied.

"I'd like to go, but I've never been on a mission trip before." His face lit up with excitement. I felt he was digesting deep in his soul that this would be the ultimate way to give to the least and the lost. Ralph thrived on giving to those who had less.

He treated everyone the same. Oh, I know. You've heard people say that about others before. One of the best ways to really see if that's true is by whom a person invites into his or her own home. Ralph loved parties. He opened his house for all kinds of gatherings and BBQs. If you happened to stop by, you were invited. When you went into his home, everyone up and down the tax bracket was there. You wouldn't know rich from poor. He loved them all.

As our conversation in the backyard ended, I asked if he would take a walk with me and talk. I sensed questions from him that needed more time for reflection. Today would be a great day. Sadly, he took a rain check. "I'll call you. I got some things I would like to talk to you about."

I went on my way and never saw him again.

Days went by that turned into several weeks. No call. I thought I would go and see him. Go by his house and pay a visit. Just talk. I never did. Not going is one of my deepest regrets.

If I had, what would have been talked about?

Would it have changed the path of Ralph over the next few weeks?

Not sure. But I think about it so often, especially when I pass his house and see no Ralph waving back to me.

Have you ever wished you had a conversation with someone and didn't? You put it off and now they're gone? Perhaps they're still around, and you're still contemplating on seeing them or not? You never know how your words may change something within them and help answer their unresolved questions.

What I would give to have that talk now.

I received a call on a Sunday morning from one of my other neighbors. He asked if I had heard.

"Heard what?" I asked.

"Chip, Ralph was killed last night. He was out late coming home and stopped for something at the local store."

I could not catch my breath. I was in shock. He went on to say that Ralph got out of his truck to look underneath because of something he heard or felt. When he did, the truck slipped out of gear and ran over the top of him. I felt sick.

He was gone.

I would never have that talk with him.

I never called just to remind him to take that walk…thinking I had time.

Have you been there? You should have called and didn't, and now it's too late?

I went to a gathering of friends and family in his honor at the local coffee shop. Person after person stood up and told of how Ralph helped them in their greatest time of need. Tears ran off my cheeks. A picture of Ralph was propped up behind each person that spoke. If anyone had a smile that could stop you in your tracks, it was Ralph. He could change your day with his smile.

Finally, Ralph's siblings spoke. It was emotional to watch as they reflected all the way back to his childhood, to what made Ralph just plain Ralph. I learned so much more. I wish I would have known those things when he was alive.

His brother reflected on the funeral. How it was a perfect tribute to Ralph's life, a person gone too soon. As he talked about the actual burial after the service, he mentioned something very interesting to me. I said, "What happened at the burial?"

He looked at the two sisters of Ralph, all of them retracing their steps that day, and said, "Did you see all the bluebirds that were at his funeral? They were everywhere. I have never seen so many bluebirds in my life."

As I choked back the lump in my throat, I recalled Ralph and his bluebird story. They showed up. The bluebirds were there. Ralph is now in a place where dreams come true. It's a place where the unimaginable becomes real. It's a place so fitting for Ralph. Ralph had passed on to another world, a world where the faithful in Christ go. He was now home, waiting for the rest of us to join him.

What is sometimes hard to understand is that he would not come back if given the choice, trust me.

He is content in Christ.

He is home forever.

He is waiting for us to have that conversation that will never end.

In the meantime, he has plenty of company.

He has all the bluebirds nesting in his backyard.

SEEKING THE THIN PLACES...

1. **Who have you lost touch with that you would like to go back and reconnect with?** Why?

2. **What conversation and with whom still plays in your mind over and over?** Why?

Entry #17

Are You All-In?

When God speaks, oftentimes His voice
will call for an act of courage on our part.

—Charles Stanley

I wanted to end this book with a story that cuts deep within all of us. It applies to all of us. It has the sting to shake up all of us. We, each one of us, can step into this scenario. Why? Because sometime, somewhere we have all stepped into this kind of predicament. To go "all-in" or not.

Remember: God is in control. No matter

how bad,

how good,

how skeptical,

how disillusioned,

how dark things may be or become,

God is overseeing all of it.

But to experience this deeply, there is one major requirement. There is no way around it. It's a question we have to ask ourselves.

Are we all-in?

With God, there is never halfway. If 100 percent is not what you're willing to do, then some other path of failure awaits you. I can say this because if it's not God's way, it leads to destruction.

I recall my football coach saying if you play with the attitude not to get hurt, you'll get hurt. But if you play as if there's no tomorrow, the game will take care of itself. In a sense, that's the way of God. If you play this game of life not to take risks, always staying on the sidelines, no intentions of trying to be more than you can imagine, pushing yourself beyond only where God can take you, why play?

I have been amazed at the size of viewership that a group of card players around a high-stakes poker table betting huge sums of money has. It seems like the latest craze. You now can play this poker online. It has huge ratings and is adding to those ratings week by week. I must admit, having never played cards, I know absolutely nothing about poker. I watched a segment of it several months ago, gasping at the pot in the middle of the table. Hundreds of thousands of dollars being thrown around like monopoly money. The only difference—you received more than two hundred dollars to pass go. In fact, to stay in a hand required thousands just to get cards dealt to you.

It takes nerves of steel. You need a face that never lets the others see you sweat. You also need to know when to get in with more money and when to take your lumps and get out. One of the most intense times during this poker game is when two people feel they have the hand to win and one utters the earthshaking words, "I'm all-in." It has a scent of finality to it. For some it is. If they lose, they're done. If they win, then they just collected one of the largest pots you can imagine. But what strikes me about this is almost every time someone utters those words, "All-in," they stand up, anticipating the next card to be shown, determining their fate.

Are they still in the game or are they going home? The next card will tell you. Your future at this table is riding on it. Who knows? I'm sure some professional players could give you odds on what the next card could possibly be. After all, their professionals, right?

Much about following God is about being all-in. It takes nerves of steel. It asks you to risk it all. It says to you, "If you lose this pot, are you still with me?" It challenges you to persevere no matter what the outcome. The difference? If you lose a hand with God, you don't have to go home. In fact, that's part of the process. You may lose the hand, but what you learned in the process is unfathomable. Always keep in mind:

God is doing the dealing.

God is in control.

Not just of this hand but of the ultimate hand we call "life."

All of us are playing whether you know it or not. You're sitting at the table and your future is resting in the middle with all the other chips on the table. You play every day. Sometimes the pot is small, sometimes the pot is large. If you make decisions each day, you're playing. Most of us have settled into a routine, satisfied with whatever tomorrow brings. We try to keep hold of our lives, hoping we can safely keep what we have. But what's the point? To come to the end of life wishing we could have done more with ourselves?

God says "If you cling to your life, you will lose it, and if you let your life go, you will save it" (Luke 17:33 NLT).

Sounds opposite to everything the world promotes. Lose it and you'll find it? Makes no sense at all. The sum of this in the end is you're not betting all that much because you're not sure of what you have. Your life seems dismal at best.

Routine has settled in like stagnant water collecting in a lifeless pond. Every day looks the same.

But what if?

What if you decided to trust God with your future? Scares you, doesn't it? You better believe it scares me. But risk and faith believe that something is going to happen even though I can't see a thing. And what happens is for my benefit, no matter what.

Leave all the consequences to God.

If you step up by putting your life in the middle and say, "I'm all-in," then get ready! You've just opened the door for God to bless you in ways you never imagined.

Let's be real. It takes courage. You have to walk the high wire without a safety net in swirling winds. God wants you to put the most important thing—*your* most important thing—in His hands. He wants your life there! To trust Him with the most prized possession you may own. To trust Him concerning a job that you feel has your future hanging in the balance.

To give God something you care nothing about or could live without requires no risk. You lose it, you lose it. That's why God said to sacrifice the purest, most unblemished lamb in the flock. Why? Because it costs something. To sacrifice something that means nothing to you is no sacrifice at all.

What if you put something in the middle that meant everything to you? Would you do it?

Several years ago, I was at a crossroad. I had to go one way or the other. I had to trust or not. Make the leap or get of the swing set. A group of us felt that God was calling us to put up a church in the southern part of the city. No big deal. We had the people, the location picked, the times and what kind of service it would be, the music to be played, all the logistics. All these decisions were made on a superficial basis. Not much faith required—just check off the boxes of what to do for a church plant to begin and off we go.

I can guess what you're thinking. It does require faith and prayer. Sure it does, and we thought and prayed about all of these things. But something needed to be done in order for this plant to move forward. I needed to move to where the church plant was going to be.

"Out of the question! I can't move. My father built this house. God wouldn't want me to sell this in order to do that."

In fact, my father and mother died in that house. It was a prized possession that carried sentimental value that I couldn't part with. Why should a church plant and its success depend on the selling of this house? That's the question, right? The house and its location had nothing to do with the church, right?

The problem was much deeper than that.

You see, if you asked one of the guys at the poker table if there were chips in his hand that he just couldn't bet, he most likely wouldn't play. If he did, he would have to play the game differently. *Handicapped* would be the better word. To have chips in your stack that you can't play with makes no sense.

Let's step into this question.

What do you have in your life that you won't let anyone handle or take control of?

Is there something that's off limits to everyone, including God?

It belongs to you and you can't part with it?

Think…think…got it?

Do you know what it is?

Now the bonus question: Has this "whatever it is" kept you from moving in the direction God wants for your life? If it has, and you now know what it is, the best advice I can give you is to learn to turn it loose. If you don't, something will always be absent in your life that may be the very key to who you are.

For me, it was the house I grew up in. I identified all my history and past with this house. I never knew it until I was asked to sell it. It became the idol of my possessions. You remember God said in the first commandment, "You shall have no other gods before me" (Exod. 20:3 NIV). Well, I had a big one. The house. I struggled and I struggled. My hand wouldn't release this one big chip in the pile. I was not willing to let it go for the purposes of something God wanted in my life that led to something better. I didn't say something bigger; I said something better. My wife hammered me over this decision. I begged God if there was any other way.

"*Nope.*" That's all I heard.

"*Let it go.*"

In *The Book of Revelation, Unlocking the Future*, Edward Hindson writes, "It is difficult, if not impossible, for most modern Christians to comprehend what it must be like to risk all you have for Christ."[1]

That's being all-in. Risking it all. The house, my house, had no value to anyone else but me. If it has value to the point of dominating space and moving God to anything less than number one, I needed to get rid of it. It was time to step up and stop playing games.

The time came when I reluctantly caved. I called the Realtor and put the house on the market. It killed me. I was so focused on the childhood home that

---

1   Edward Hindson, *The Book of Revelation, Unlocking the Future* (Chattanooga, TN: AMG Publishers, 2002), 37.

the church plant still took a backseat. My attitude was, how can I keep it and still look like I'm trying to get rid of it? To the neighbors, it must have seemed strange. Cheery and I were now living in another house where the church plant was to be and calls came in to buy the house. But there was still a heart issue. God sees the heart. God knows when you're bluffing; God knows when you're serious. Imagine having God play your hand at the poker table. How unfair but prosperous that would be.

I had failed to do one thing: to put a sign in the yard that said, "For Sale." I couldn't do it. It seemed so final. But I must tell you, nothing was going right until I put the sign in the yard. Sounds silly, I'm sure, but seriously, it all came down to the sign. The sign represented a house for sale. *The* house. What it really read to me on the sign was, "All-In."

God wants all of you or nothing. Sounds brutal, right? Who demands this kind of loyalty? Your work? Your school? Your marriage? You could make a case for all three, but this is something entirely different. I mean every inch of you God desires. But here is the main difference. Your work, your school, and your marriage are dependent on human interaction with others, no matter how you slice it. I think it's fair to say they don't have your best interests in mind. They have *their* best interests in mind. God puts us first in all things, while expecting us to give Him our best. Our all. Our houses. He wants us to put the sign up and be willing to let it all go.

Now, here's the kicker.

Guess what happened once I put the sign in the yard? One evening in the other house, my wife and I were having dinner. Quiet and calm. No TV. No radio playing. Only the voice of God on the inside whispering to our spirits.

"Time to go home."

Did you get that? We both looked at each other and right in the middle of eating, we looked up and heard the same thing.

"*Time to go home.*"

We got giggly and silly over the course of several minutes. She asked me and I asked her, "Do you hear and feel what I am hearing and feeling?" We didn't know what to do. This house was full of all our things. We just moved three months ago. Now what? God can't be serious? We laughed again. Could we move back? Go back to the home that I always felt I could never sell? Why would we spend so much time at moving, only to up and go back? I can only think of one word when you decide to be all-in:

Obedience!

Sometimes the end result is not what God is thinking about. It may turn out good at the time, or it may not. But know God cannot work in your life unless He has all of you. To hand over your life to Him requires obedience. Total obedience. Total surrender.

The thin place for me is God having me realize that to find my life I need to be on the same page and the same agenda He is on. God is in control. God comes first. Not the house. Funny thing, though. Not until the sign went in the yard did God know in my heart I was willing to turn it loose.

What about you?

Do you have something in your life that seems on the outside as if you are being obedient but the heart still is holding chips in the corner you refuse to release?

I think of all the personalities in Scripture whose lives, if they had not risked it all, would have never been blessed. Nor would they have realized what lay within them to do great things. Perhaps the greatest point to remember is this:

When you're obedient, when you're all-in, God is responsible for your life, not you. That takes all the pressure off you.

HE is the compass,

HE is the provider,

HE is comforter,

HE will set you up for success, not failure.

But you have to have the courage to hang in when your cards look dismal and all your chips are in the middle of the pot. Do you trust God? Do you trust God when everything looks bleak? If you can do this, you are in great company.

Moses

Abraham

Joseph

Esther

Remember Christ's first call to each of His disciples? Maybe they were all scared. God took control of their lives. They often questioned, and they rarely understood what Christ was doing. But they never looked back.

History was written with them in mind. They were all-in when most would have folded.

Live your life all-in.

God will do some miraculous things in the thin places of your life, if you're just willing to take the journey.

Be blessed. My prayer for you is that one day we could meet and share a story or two. Life is about stories. Jesus was the greatest storyteller ever. His stories and life changed the world. Go be a part of it in these thin places.

SEEKING THE THIN PLACES...

1. Concerning you personally, what does it mean to be "all-in"?

2. What is the hardest thing for you to turn over to God?

3. Why is this "thing" so important to you?

4. What sacrifices would you need to make, what changes in your personhood would have to be altered, for you to give God total control of your life?

The Climb

(A Ministry Resource Organization)

Christ Like
In Mind and Body

CLIMB'S vision is to model ministry, train leaders, and be a catalyst to help reach people for Christ based on their culture and their needs. It's all about people and their potential.

CLIMB dreams of encouraging and equipping people to release their God-given potential to change the world for Christ.

CLIMB'S mission is to help develop community centers in needy nations where children can gather, learn, and play in a safe and loving environment; where adults can learn a marketable skill; where local church leaders can get up-to-the-minute seminary type training; where mission teams can base their operations serving the local community in medical, leadership training and construction missions. The nondenominational center will serve the entire community, Christian and non-Christian; saved and not yet saved.

CLIMB is presently in the process of opening a nonprofit coffee house in Charlotte, NC, for the purpose of supporting the building of community centers in needy nations throughout our hemisphere.

If you would like to know more about CLIMB's ministry efforts, the incredible results we are experiencing, become a prayer partner, or perhaps become a fan or supporter, contact us at www.theclimb.org.

If You're a Fan of This Book, Please Tell Others . . .

- Write about *Thin Places* on your blog, Twitter, MySpace, or Facebook page.

- Suggest *Thin Places* to friends.

- When you're in a bookstore, ask them if they carry the book. The book is available through all major distributors, so any bookstore that does not have *Thin Places* in stock can easily order it.

- Write a positive review of *Thin Places* on www.amazon.com.

- Send my publisher, HigherLife Publishing, suggestions on Web sites, conferences, and events you know of where this book could be offered. Please email HigherLife Publishing at media@ahigherlife.com.

- Purchase additional copies to give away as gifts. Books can be ordered through our Web site at www.theclimb.org. Of course, you can purchase the book on Amazon or through any major bookstore, but it helps our ministry most when you order directly through our Web site.

Tell Me About Your Own
Thin Place Encounter...

Life is full of thin places. There's a narrow line between life and death, peace and war, success and failure, walking with God or being oblivious to His presence. Hopefully as you have read this book, your own soul has been awakened to the reality and promise that there are thin places all around you every day! I'd love to hear your story. Who knows, you could make it into my next book (only with your approval, of course). To write about your own thin place, please visit my blog at www.chipfurr.org. You may also e-mail me directly at chip@theclimb.org.